Eon

[handwritten, illegible]

and you have an

exciting ...

WHEN? WHERE? WHY?

A History of the Wars and Conflicts We Have Fought

by

Edward Brittingham

Capt E W Brittingham

3-29-19

RoseDog ❧ Books
PITTSBURGH, PENNSYLVANIA 15238

RoseDog Books
585 Alpha Drive, Suite 103
Pittsburgh, PA 15238
Visit our website at *www.rosedogbookstore.com*

ISBN: 978-1-4809-7722-8
eISBN: 978-1-4809-7699-3

REVIEWS

"The majority of books and documents concentrate on small isolated historical events. Important... yes...entertaining....usually; however, they are just small pieces of the big puzzle we refer to as history.

Captain Brittingham's "When? Where ? Why ?": is one of those rare books that takes a step back, looks at the major pieces of the puzzle and then pulls them together to show the big picture."

Kenneth Swell, Author: "All Hands Down:
The True Story of the Soviet Attack on the USS Scorpion"

"When? Where? Why?: are right in line with countries woes and a very sad commentary on what our great nation has become and the future appears darker than ever.

Several years ago I wrote a novel, based on many journalistic encounters I endured when talking with politicians, titled Any Thing but the Truth. The story points out the fact that when a politician, at any level of government, is asked "what color is the sky", rather than say it's blue, they will tell you how many different shades of blue one can get by manipulating a color wheel.

When? Where? Why?: shines an even greater spotlight on the manipulation of facts as used by politicians throughout the twentieth century and continues into the twenty-first."

Art Giberson, Author: "The Mighty O; U.S.S. Oriskany CVA 34

"When? Where? Why?, presents Mike Brittingham's look at the growth political correctness over the past decades and focuses on the unclouded reality of events on the last 8 years under President Obama."

Captain Richard W. Michaux, USN, (Ret)

Contents

Last, but by no means least, courage—moral courage, the courage of one's convictions, the courage to see things through. The world is in a constant conspiracy against the brave. It's the age-old struggle—the roar of the crowd on one side and the voice of your conscience on the other.

General Douglas McArthur

DEDICATION

As we travel to military bases book signing we are amazed at the people who serve, active duty, workers, housekeepers, and personnel at the exchanges. We dedicate this book to you who have enriched our lives and many of you have become our friends. To all who wear, or have worn the uniform we thank you, in memory of all who died for our country. Thank each of you.

A special thanks to Carol Mackey who has been my computer technician and volunteered to type the entire book by herself and to my loving wife Joyce whose love and support are invaluable to me.

FOREWORD BY JOYCE BRITTINGHAM

My husband gave 23½ years of honorable service to his country before suffering a massive stroke, the effects he still lives with today. When I met and married him twenty-four years later, I know him to be a man of honor, a man of his word, and a man of faith. I am proud to be his wife, lover, and share a wonderful live together.

I have watched him research material for his books, fill legal pads, and yes type (with one hand!) but the most fun is book signing at Barnes & Noble Book Stores and military bases all over the east coast. Such wonderful people we meet from "top brass" to enlisted men, employees at the exchanges and the housekeeping ladies who I have made lasting friendships with.

To all who have thanked him for his service and shook his hand I say, Thank You!!

PREFACE

Memorial Day is a Federal Holiday in the United States of America which remembers the men and woman who lost their lives serving in the Armed Forces. This holiday is celebrated on the last Monday in May. Decoration Day is another way of expressing this event. This occasion originated after the Civil War or The War Between The States which honor and sacrifice to the Union and Confederate soldiers who perished during this war.

Many people decorate their graves at cemeteries with poppies or other festive flowers. Most volunteers place an American flag which is usually done in National Cemeteries.

Memorial Day is not to be confused with Veterans Day! Memorial Day remembers the men and woman who died while serving, yet Veterans Day celebrates the service of all U. S. Veterans.

Over the past 150 years we have brought our service men and woman through utter damnation participating in many battles in which our homeland is at stake – The Civil War in 1860 – 1865; World War I 1914 – 1918, and World War II 1940 – 1945. Remember that fateful day when Pearl Harbor was attacked by Japan. The Korean War, 1950 – 1953, in which our country had not built a ship since 1946!

The Vietnam War 1959 – 1975, this is the 54th anniversary of this major conflict! As I quote, "We reflect with solemn reverence upon the valor of a generation that served with honor. We pay tribute to 3 million service men and women who left their families so bravely. From Ia Drang to Khe Sanh, from Hue to Saigon and countless villages in between; they pushed through jungles and rice paddies, heat and monsoons, fighting heroically to protect the ideals that we hold so dear as

Americans! After more than a decade of combat, over air, land and sea, these proud Americans uphold the highest traditions of our Armed Forces."

In 1973 a call was received from Washington, D.C. The Casualty Assistance Calls Office (CACO) for a missing A-6 pilot in North Vietnam. The wife was visited and I kept her in my thoughts for over a year.

85,000 patriots, the names etched in black granite – who had served all that had and will ever know in Vietnam. Incidentally, the statue of Abraham Lincoln is looking down on this awesome site in Washington, D.C.

Missing in action, MIA, they are still looking for clues. But the statistics for World War II break down to 78,750 MIA which is 19% of the total perished. Vietnam there are 2,255 unaccounted for which equates to 4% of 58,152 killed.

In this cemetery or any place of rest, where we are standing, they are at peace – those who have honored all the conflicts including Desert Storm, Iraq, and Afghanistan. This is not complete but ISIS is another struggle in which we have started to participate. In all of the problems and the events of the past, we must remember the loss of the brave! Remember each of your dead as one of your loved ones! When the funeral calls for me, my wife will share under a gravestone at Arlington National Cemetery in Arlington, Virginia.

God bless America!

PROLOGUE

With a loud bolter of noise of the television, the news announces the various headlines. My morning coffee brings some sanatorium to the news advocated by Fox News. If it is not the Republican debate last week or not, the aggressive blaze of the president explaining an instance of absurd action with the Iran/United States agreement which has been decided in September 2015. Nevertheless the agreement of our Planned Parenthood plus the drastic cities that have suffered murders, riots, and misuse of the police causing chaotic racist actions in many cities.

On the other side of the net, Hillary Clinton is running for the Democratic president plus three other candidates. Although the Clinton Clan has forgotten the raging Benghazi incident of September 11, 2012, and left the door open for answers. The lies and other actions by President Obama, Hillary Clinton, and Susan Rice (the president's National Security advisor), were full of prevarication and very monstrous! The derivation of truth, the use of Benghazi's real happenings, and the Obama administration pretended the attack had nothing to indicate terrorism. Hillary Clinton and the president are targeted for frank explanation on how this diabolicalness reared its ugly head! Not only the Ambassador plus three others in Benghazi, their killings were unanswered yet several others lost their lives protecting the compound and the Central Intelligence Agency in Libya. Yet the Secretary of State refusing to sign the release of secret documents has uncovered a blazing strife! Her president polls while running, regarding its ratings, have continually fallen during her predicted race.

The other side of the world laughs at President Obama and his neglect of his foreign policy. His laughable trip several years ago brought many mistakes throughout England, Germany, Egypt, Iran, Saudi Arabia, and Russia, Vladimir Putin. This does not mean he visited these countries but all turned a sour note to the United States' foreign policy or lack of.

So today we are faced with critical problems which may cause possible Iran getting a nuclear bomb while ISIS is happier than a grown caliphate!

INTRODUCTION

What is war – a conflict or a state of hostility? We don't grasp the agony of self-sacrifice of a state of open and declared armed conflict among the states or nations. The endgame is that one destroys or weakens the other side. My six books have covered various stages of struggle/war, including the present. Speaking with many thousands of customers, I have surmised that the overall population does not have a clue of the details of war! In essence, as a generation, we are in the envelope of guessing, wondering what war or terrorism can do to a country, nation, or the entire world.

This book begins one hundred years ago with the start of World War I. Each encounter is tested, and each act bears another factor which can influence the outcome. The inevitable end is the vast amount of terrorist bands which can be contained or they threaten the United States of America.

CHAPTER 1: WORLD WAR I

THE WAR TO END WARS 1914-1918

OVERVIEW

Looking date after date, we settle on one hundred years – the beginning of 1914, the World War I. The actual conflict began in Europe, which led to the countries as far away as Japan and the United States. "The Great War" it was called by the English-speaking generally. This controversy led to whether it was "blowing smoke," it was not due to the degree of opinions. The period commencing the build-up of the war was a debate of strategies or battle plans which created havoc! Inevitably, the war was chaotic and downright perplexed. Historians unanimously agreed about the conflict's final outcome. World War I brought about World War II which set in force an audible whisper for significant happenings in the twentieth century.

By conservative guesses, about nine million soldiers lost their lives – many defending front lines that inevitably moved to either side no more than several yards. Civilian losses totaled nine million, with epidemics of other diseases reaching twenty million, either induced or caused by violence evidently caused by the war.

Government tensions were critical in this period, as Europe's powers were becoming great with the appointment of several colonies. Turkey ruled the Ottoman Empire, which had become convenient during the last several hundred years, but was showing signs of deterioration. Greece, Bulgaria, Romania and other southern nations that had been under the Ottoman Empire had suddenly become independent. This obviously changed the balance of power among these countries, energizing the many ethnic groups in Austria-Hungary which inspired and agitated for their own independent political unit.

Meanwhile, technological vis-a-vis industrial gains in Europe were moving ahead at an impressive speed. Military advancements using improved weapons only promised a horrible war. World War I would be an exhibit of new engineering that would change the nature, speed and efficiency of war to come. The employment of tanks, airplanes and submarines changed the way warfare vaulted in the coming war. Motorized vehicles, cars, tanks, trains, have speed to capitalize the speed which troops and supplies are rapidly supplied. Guns, all types, increased in accuracy and range of fire have a quarter distances to effect killing the enemy. The machine gun, which can take out multiple targets at once and the use of chemical weapons; warrants a gruesome army which some countries have showed not to use this poison gas again.

By war's end, the map of countries real remained the same, almost. The Germans and Austro-Hungarians went away. Most of the countries around were subdivided and some left independent countries. A major reorganization establishes the settlements of countries we know today as Armenia, Turkey, Syria, Lebanon, Saudi Arabia and Iraq.

European colonialism and the practical end of monarchy over the world was brought to an end at the end of the war. Most European nations began to rely on parliamentary elements of government, including outbreaks of socialism.

TOP FIVE CAUSES OF WWI

At the end of WWI on November 11, 1918, over 100,000 American troops were lost. As a result of the scrimmage, this brought out the complexity of warfare other than the simple engagement techniques. Root causes of this war were much deeper than envisioned, but these pertained to the fighting.

MUTUAL DEFENSE ALLIANCES

Many countries were pulled into the conflict which showed mutual defense agreements found themselves in battle, the following nations were bonded by agreements:

- Russia and Serbia
- Germany and Austria-Hungary
- France and Russia
- Brittan, France and Belgium

• Japan and Britain

Austria-Hungary was at war with Serbia, Russia defended Serbia. Germany seeing Russia getting ready for battle became at war with Russia. France was brought into the war and Germany attacked them through Belgium by pulling Britain into the conflict. Japan entered the war and later Italy and the United States entered the war on the side of the Allies.

IMPERIALISM

Imperialism is a nation that influences its power by including other territories by control. Africa and others were particularity interested in the many raw materials they could supply. The many efforts by mature countries to capture vast assets brought the empires that helped them pushed the world to war.

MILITARISM

The twentieth century brought the arms race. Germany in 1914 was the leader in the buildup of the military; Great Britain and German were building ships at a record pace. This increase in militarism caused a vital push to help countries involved in WWI.

NATIONALISM

Much of the war involved whether the Slavic people in Bosnia and in Herzegovina were to be a part not of Austria, Hungary but to belong to Serbia. Nationalism led to the Great War, yet this pontificate to various countries in Europe often counteracted not only to the outbreak of war but the extension of war in Europe. Each country provided its own power to people their dominance.

Inevitable Cause: Assassination of Archduke Franz Ferdinand.

The primary cause of this war was the aforementioned items, for example, alliance imperialism, militarism, etc., so was the assassination of Archduke Franz Ferdinand mover of Austria-Hungary in June 1914.

The Black Hand, a Serbian terrorist group, sent news to kill the archduke. The first attempt failed but Gavrilo Princip killed both husband and wife in Sarajevo, Bosnia, in Austria-Hungary. The killing denied making control of Serbia and wanted control of Bosnia and Herzegovina. This horrendous massacre led to Austria-Hungary at war on Serbia. Germany anointed it and archived war on Russia, and eventually all nations, also it seems, declared war with mutual defiance alliance.

THE WORLD WAR I

With the assassination of Archduke Franz Ferdinand the war commenced with little shock or surprise. Assassination of heads was unlikely. They descended with troops was unlikely yet Europe had been at peace for most half a century.

The main players were France, German, Italy, Russia, Austria-Hungary, Turkey and Britain.

Within the context, there were three wild cards, slow nationalism; the second was Austria-Hungary which averted Serbian national courage. The wildest card was the German emperor, Kaiser Wilhelm II. He fired Otto von Bismarck and constructed an unbelievable amount of armed forces. When the British built the powerful battleship the dreadnought, he ordered a version of a battleship that was twice the British version. The battle would come later!

Even the USA, now a Pacific as well as Atlantic contender of power had annexed Hawaii as well as the Philippines from Spain. This appears as a mighty asset for the country a valid force in the coming war.

Since the balance was tipped and all atrocities were open, all countries began to mobilize offering a draft of soldiers to the country of battle.

Warfare has changed in the event; killing was a pledge of imagination. New technology was called in, a new weapon or weapons, has informed or altered the death rates.

Fighting in the trenches offered left struggling in the made only one thousand yards away from the enemy. The gas attack was next on the shelf. This causes deaths without a standardized gas mask and causes injury a soldier may never inflict on the enemy. In addition with discussions the invention of the tank, various influx of new guns, and the battle of the airplanes and the conflict of the battleships brought new ideas.

The tank was first used in 1914. They used the tank as more of an armed caterpillar-traction used to land troops over iron barriers behind the tank. One tank burst into flowers with another a British Mark V in 1918 used his weapon to drive and clear the area with machine gun fire.

The machine gun was the potent arsenal of the trenches. All commanders in German, Russia or whatever; this was a valid tactic. The battle of the airplane was instrumental in the early 1915 when a German scout falls from a basket that was placed on a balloon. The battle of the airplane evolved from the airplane to airships. The first airplane flew in 1900 and it vastly overtook the airship with Germany building over one hundred planes.

By 1918, the Zeppelins took charge by dropping bombs and were becoming vulnerable to the explosive bullets which turned their hydrogen-rich environment into burning flames! In 1915, the Fokker correlated the engine propeller to fire through the tuning propeller. From this idea came the world famous pilot, "Red Baron." He was killed in a fire promoted by the Royal Air Force.

The surface fleet was mighty during the war. In the beginning, there was Britain and Germany. The lord of the ocean, Sir John Fisher, guessed that his kings of the sea would unleash Armageddon – this was never accomplished!

The United States suffered a great loss when the German U-boat sank the Lusitania on May 7, 1915. The Lusitania was a 31,000 ton Canard liner left Norfolk on its way to Liverpool, England.

The sinking caused a loss of 173 tons of rifles and ammunition. A total of 1,198 people were lost as the ship was diving in the depths of the sea.

The British cruiser Hampshire was hit by a German mine. The American navy was the first American troops will seat 14,000 of men arrived in France in 1917. America, now involved in the war, sent many convoys, airplanes, men and tanks into the war.

On June 28, 1919, the treaty was signed by the Germans. This offered a series of Germany refusals to sign, which granted a number of military forces which infuriated the German officials. Finally, the agreement was agreed whose delegates had been held in embarrassing conditions. When the peace agreement was signed, the German delegation returned to the fatherland and produced a new constitution for Germany.

WORLD WAR I – ITS MISTAKES

1. The End of the German Fleet – The Versailles treaty being signed the German fleet would be sunk. The first to detonate the ocean floor was French Admiral Comte de Grasse. The rest followed with the last to sink was Hindenburg. The four remaining ships were towed ashore by British ships. This act left Germany a weak, hungry nation without a valid ship defense.

2. The renewal offensive in 1915 fell short of achieving an effort to end the war. Either effort was stymied and led to regrouping of either side.

3. Battles involving trench lines, air power, and fighting. World War I was exhausting and degrading while Germany lost the summer to fall back to the offensive force.

4. The plague of influenza broke out during the war. This took heavy tolls on soldiers on either side of the conflict.

5. The governments of German and Austria-Hungary lost control of both countries as both lost multiple mutinies within their military structure.

6. Germany after The War – Historians believe that we were too excessive in their treatment of German at the outcome of World War I. The Treaty of Versailles actually grew the seeds of World War II! Ultimately the extremist groups, the Nazi Party, began to take political control of the country which led to World War II.

7. In the nature of war, the aircraft is an important entity. Use the aircraft to launch an attack on land, but bombs make a disastrous difference.

8. The League of Nations of WWI has finally been reborn.

The United Nations and American have accepted their role of influence demanded by President Wilson's principles of reconciliation and cooperation. Only then will years pass until it be said that the supreme death of over eight million lives have not been in vain.

CHAPTER 2: WORLD WAR II

DIPLOMACY IN WORLD WAR II

TRYING TO STAY OUT OF THE GOOD WAR

It would pass that the "Good War" was one conflict that almost everyone agrees that these battles were worth fighting. In modern American history, this was one war at the time that did not support joining. Even the three worse wars Korea, Vietnam and Iraq all enjoyed greater public support than our entry into WW II.

This was by far the largest conflict in history documented by spanning the globe or world as well as the creation of new weapons including nuclear bombs.

Not all countries participated in the war, however; some were involved in supplying arms and others items that were used by both nations. For example, the D-Day date was decided by a congregation of nations. Ireland supplied weather data in conjunction with Sweden and Switzerland assisted General Dwight Eisenhower in the go-ahead of Normandy or D-Day.

World War II ravaged civilians, unthinkable in any previous conflict and served as a backdrop for the genocidal killings by Germany. Other slaughters of civilian personnel were significant, the massacre of Chinese and Korean nationals by Japan, internal killings led the Soviet Union, and the bombing of civilian targets by the Allied bombers. In total, the war produced 50 million deaths, the most of any war.

Late in the summer of 1940, a year after the war began, Adolph Hitler began his blitzing annihilation of Poland. A full 80% of the American people polled by George Gallup that they would vote "no" if the uncertainty of USA was to enter the conflict would be brought to a referendum!

7

By the time the United States joined in December 1941, a furious proclamation to Japan's surprise attach of December 7, 1941. Hawaii – China had been fighting Japan for four and a half years. The British had been at war for two years fighting the Germans. This was a result of an attempt to create a fascist empire. The Soviet Union was fighting the advances of Germany, who was set to run over Joseph Stalin. America's late entry into this war came as a godsend to the Allies. These belligerent countries marked the first years of battle as setbacks and endless defeats.

DIVERGENT ROADS TO WAR

The road to hostile conflict was not a straight or narrow path. These roads lead to war, each leading to a separate path to war, until the paths diverged in a different direction, they merged at Pearl Harbor. The first and primary mission was Adolf Hitler aggressively pushed the nations toward war. Second was a roadblock or detour with the United States doing everything possible for not participating in the conflict. And the third reason was US President Franklin Roosevelt slowly maneuvering this country in support of the Allies despite rising public support. This caused a series of restrictive laws that demanded strict neutrality.

RESPONDING TO HITLER WITH NEUTRALITY

President Franklin Roosevelt began his presidential tour with the Great Depression in 1933. Unfortunately, this was the bleakest winter in history. In less than three weeks, Nazi leader Adolf Hitler became dictator of Germany. In other words, the same economic downturn fueled the election of Roosevelt as well as boosting Hitler to supreme power.

The re-emergence of Germany and the establishing of a military draft violated the Versailles Treaty. The Neutrality Act of 1935 was established by the U.S. Congress plus Britain and France. This act provided to block release of weapons related to war items to any party or to any foreign agent. Not only the president could not disturb war minded items to other war countries, Roosevelt was growing unsure with the downfall of the Nazi measure he signed the bill into law. Therefore, the hideous of Nazi regime unfolded for five years, since this bill became law.

FROM NAZI OLYMPICS TO THE RAPE OF NANKING

Early in 1936, Congress passed a censure law that forbid transactions with foreign nations in addition to a ban on military aid, Hitler moved his army to Rhineland where he moved to a region near the German / French border. The United States sent a sizable group to the world Olympic Games in Berlin, Germany. The event that sealed the American presence in Berlin was the African-American sprinter Jesse Owens. Owens crushed the superior "white" athletics, winning four gold medals before capturing cheering German crowds. This totally embarrassed Adolph Hitler's views, a most abashing assertion! As an aside, 1936 was dedicated as 95% opposed to the American people in entering a military confrontation in Europe.

World War II began in Japan when it invaded China in 1937. China at that time was an ally. Stories in the west about Japanese hostilities, such as atrocities such as rape, mass murder and this was called the Rape of Nanking. Interesting enough, six percent favored against Japan wanted military intervention against that country staying in China. This caused another neutrality act even stronger than before.

AMERICANS BACK NEVILLE CHAMBERLAIN
"PEACE FOR OUR TIME"

In 1938 Hitler's malevolent plans were impossible to escape, they swallowed up Austria. In six months' time he demanded that Czechoslovakia hand over Switzerland. Though Czechoslovakia was ready for battle, the French leaders joined British Prime Minister Neville Chamberlin by going to Munich to negotiate a peaceful agreement. By helping the Nazi leader go along with this plan, they allowed Germany to seize Sudetenland in exchange for a worthless promise that the agreement would settle all differences. Chamberlain returned to London pleased with what had transpired! But his confidence was broken; his argument was tragically misguided by the German Right! Neville Chamberlain is remembered as one of the most despised and least thought of public figures in the twentieth century. Funny, 59% of the American people believed he had done the best thing – giving into Germany instead of going to war.

KRISTALLNACHT: THE BEGINNING OF THE HOLOCAUST

In late 1938 the Nazis continued the violence against the Jews. This act of horror began by the German nation and it started by a series of discriminatory laws. In November 1938 this changed to Kristallnacht, the "Night of Broken Glass" whipped the Jews by organizing a nationwide launch against Jewish houses. Many homes and businesses were looted; smashed, many were arrested and murdered. Many Jews were arrested and were sent to concentration camps. This caused a great concern in the American people. As late as April 1939 84% of the U.S. people opposed this act of German aggression. 69% were against the lending of money to Britain and France to arm them while taking on World War II. President Roosevelt begged Congress, yet he was firmly rebuffed. Kristallnacht was the start of Jewish harassment, concentration camps and the beginning of the Second World War.

THE FALL OF POLAND AND FRANCE

Beginning on September 1939 the German offensive rolled into Poland proving Neville Chamberlain hopelessly naïve. Adolph Hitler's feverish military juggernaut of tanks rolled across Poland. France and Britain declared war which they had no other chance. Roosevelt finally won a small segment of Congress which was labeled the Neutrality Act of 1939.

The act barred shipping to those warring nations. With the treasuries of both Britain and France depleted by German submarines in the Atlantic Ocean, the "Cash and Carry" provision straddled Roosevelt's ability to help.

The war took a turn for worse in 1940, several months of "phony war" between France and Britain; however, none of the armies did actual fighting. The Germans stepped up the battle with a blitzkrieg.

German invasion of France, the soldiers of France were immediately overwhelmed. In fact, an expeditionary British force was surrendered at the French port of Dunkirk. It took civilian fishing boats or the light pleasure boats to save the British force.

Less than six weeks later, after the war began, the French government surrendered. Winston Churchill assumed as Prime Minister and promised to continue the war against Hitler or "We shall not flag or fail," Mr. Churchill proclaimed. With the new prime minister resolved, most Americans joined his alliance. In any respect he survived in the darkest days of the Second World War.

ROOSEVELT'S WAR

American President Franklin D. Roosevelt began to circumvent the restrictions of the Neutrality Act in order to provide maximum help for the British. He declared millions of ammunition and American firearms to be "surplus" to our military requirements. He sent this to England plus aging destroyers, fifty in number, to Britain. They made alliances to send convoys from U.S. and Canada to Iceland; and into England. The other trouble was sending many convoys in the Atlantic Ocean teemed with German submarines. As this problem was put into place the outbreak of Japan was obvious. December 7, 1941, was a surprise attack on the battle force in Pearl Harbor, Hawaii. The apparent lack of getting a long message through from Washington D.C., and the four carriers' transiting toward Hawaii, this was a blow to the Navy and yet there were no carriers in Pearl Harbor.

U.S. NAVY IN WORLD WAR II

The navy grew rapidly in pursuit of the war during 1941 – 1945. This conflict was no match for Japan, Germany and with the British Navy. It played a victorious role against Germany and Italy. The Navy as may be sighted began with the production started with the building of the USS North Carolina (BB-55) in 1937. The lead ship of four battleships, she took part in the offensive in the Pacific Theater of Operations. North Carolina began construction on October 27, 1937, at the New York shipyard and was launched June 13, 1940. She was the fastest battery of battleships and carried a main battery of nine 16-inch 45 caliber mark 6 guns. She was called "Showboat" during her sea trials which were excellent by far. Her propulsion systems carried her to excellence, without failure or damage to the ship.

She finally completed her shakedown cruise before the Pearl Harbor incident, she remained in the Atlantic as a potential counter against the German ship Tirpitz if she began to attack supply and other ships destined for Great Britain. By the summer of 1942, North Carolina was ordered to the Pacific Ocean. She brought her 16-inch guns with her first assignment to escort carriers. The battleship was tasked to screen the enterprise by protecting the carrier. Later protected the supply used communications to the Solomon Islands and Guadalcanal.

ICELAND

On June 16, 1941, the problem became defense of Iceland vis-a-vis the convoys leaving from Canada and stopping briefly at Iceland before continuing to England. Negotiation with Churchill and Roosevelt ordered the United States occupation of Iceland, instead of replacing the onslaught of British invasion forces. June 22, 1941, the Navy sent Task Force 19 (TF-19) from Charleston, South Carolina, to embargo and land at Argentia, Newfoundland. TF-19 included 25 warships and the first Provisional Marine Brigade with 194 officers and about 3,800 men from San Diego.

TF-19 sailed from Argentia on July 1 and British trusted the news to approve an American occupation force under an U.S.-Icelandic defense agreement. TF-19 anchored off Reykjavik, Iceland, after the voyage from Newfoundland. The U.S. Marines commenced landing and disembarkation was completed on July 12. With the arrival of Patrol Squadron VP-73 PB Marines and VP-74 PBM Marines, the

Navy established an air base at Reykjavik, Iceland. U.S. Army personnel arrived in Iceland in August and the marines were transferred to the Pacific by March 1942. Up to 40,000 U.S. military personnel were on the island outdistancing the male population of Iceland. The agreement was for the military to remain until War World II ended. In reality, the U.S. personnel remained in Iceland through 2006.

PEARL HARBOR

The Battle of Pearl Harbor was an attack or a surprise invasion that started the war with Japan. December 7, 1941, "a date which will live in infamy" was a crushing blow to our forces in place at Pearl Harbor. The attack was a profound shock to the American people which led to war in both American and European theaters.

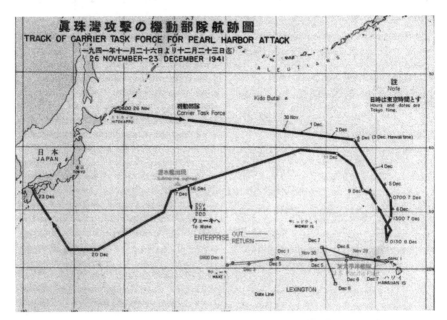

Track of Carrier Task Force – Pearl Harbor

The attack commenced at 7:48 a.m. Hawaiian time. The base was attacked by 353 Japanese fighter planes, torpedo planes and bombers, which came in several waves. The tally of ships sank or damaged three cruisers, three destroyers and our anti-submarine training ship. The principal loss was the eight battleships were damaged with four sunk. Of the United States aircraft, 188 were destroyed. Important installations such as power stations, shipyard maritime, submarine slots, and the intelligence buildings were not harmed.

The attack was agreed to commence December 7, 1941, at 0748, with planning to develop a surprise attack. The Japanese tactical forces set about numerous avenues of getting ship data, weather information, and the Navy positions of the airfields, numbers of aircraft and numerous incidents primarily for an unknown attack on Pearl Harbor. With the information streaming back to Japan, this was vital to the intelligence gurus. One of the primary means of the influx of data was on the military side. Many charts showing the harbor of Pearl Harbor and the mooring of the ships were purposely filtering in. The Japanese Naval aircraft had a tough nut to crack. The harbor where the U.S. ships are anchored is not a deep in water level in the Pacific Ocean. The torpedo that the ships use is a deep running missile. To counter this, an added piece of steel, lack of a better word, upon impact of the water, this device caught the depth of the torpedo at forty feet!

Saturday, December 6 – The president of the United States, President Franklin D. Roosevelt waits for the final appeal to the Emperor of Japan referring to the 14-part message. Finally the U.S. secret code-breaking device intercepted the 14-part Japanese message. The Americans believe a Japanese attack is imminent, therefore most likely somewhere in Southeast Asia. In Washington, D.C., the intelligence force saw the need and dedication to run the 14-part message to the higher ups.

Sunday, December 7 – Washington, D.C. – The last part of the ongoing message which proclaims that all diplomatic relations have ended. At ten o'clock in the morning another message was intercepted. The main message insists that the final part be delivered to the Americans at 1:00 p.m. Washington Eastern standard time. Finally the intelligence forces override the command which the time is well behind Pearl Harbor.

The U.S. War Department sends out an alert, but the radio contact with Hawaii was temporarily interrupted. All in all, delays prevented the radio warning arriving at Oahu until noon time Hawaii Time: four hours after the attack commenced!

Sunday, December 7 – The Islands of Hawaii, new Oahu – The Japanese attack force under command of Admiral Nagumo, consisting of six carriers, 423 aircraft was ready to launch air attack. At six o'clock a.m., 183 Japanese planes took off from carriers 230 miles north of Oahu and head for the U.S. Pacific Fleet at Pearl Harbor.

At 7:02 two army men detected the mass of aircraft headed towards the island. A junior officer acknowledged the contacts and believes they are the B-17 planes that are expected from the west coast!

Another wave of 167 planes took off at 1:15 a.m. and heads for Pearl Harbor.

Pearl Harbor was not on a state of high alert. Senior commanders based over-rated intelligence that there was the reason a surprise attack was imminent. Aircraft were parked wing tip to wing tip on airfields and unmanned anti-aircraft guns with ammunition in boxes kept locked in accordance with peacetime regulations. And, therefore, there are no torpedo nets protecting the fleet anchorage? At 7:53 a.m. the first wave of Japanese aircraft, namely 51 "Val "dive bombers, 40 "Kate" torpedo bombers, 50 high level bombers and 43 "Zero" fighters. Flight Commander Mitsuo Fuchida proceeded with a cry of "Tora! Tora! Tora (Tiger! Tiger! Tiger!)!

The Americans were caught completely by surprise! The initial attack targeted airfields and battleships. The second wave targeted other ship and facilities. The air raid lasted until 9:45 a.m. with eight battleships damaged with five sunk. Three light cruisers, destroyers, and smaller vessels including 188 aircraft. On the other side, Japan lost 27 planes and five midget submarines, which attempted to penetrate the inner harbor to launch torpedoes; escaping damage was the prime target, the carrier, the three carriers were not in port. And best of all the fuel tanks were not harmed, this was a big surprise to the Japanese Navy, which early reports confirmed it was home ported in Pearl Harbor.

News of the "sneak bombardment" was broadcast to the American public and many entertainment shows were substituted over the news of the attack. This attack bonded the President and effectively ended isolationist sentiment in the country.

Monday, December 15 – War is declared between Japan and the United States. On December 11, 1941, Germany and Italy declared war against the United States. The European and Southwest Asia have become a global conflict with the Axis powers Japan, German and Italy pitted against America, Britain, France and the Allies.

Wednesday December 17 Admiral Chester W. Nimitz becomes Commander of the U.S. Pacific Fleet. Both Commands at Pearl Harbor, Admiral Husband E. Kimmel and Army Lieutenant General Walter C. Short, were relieved of their duties following the attack. Later investigations found both men guilty for failing to adopt adequate defense measures.

WW II MIDWAY

The Battle of Midway targeted the turning point in the Pacific. Starting in June 4, 1942, the U.S. Navy defeated a Japanese naval force. The U.S. carrier fleet had foxed the Japanese by not falling into the trap at Midway Atoll. The Japanese lost four carriers to one carrier and one destroyer. After Midway and the exhausting attrition of Solomon Island campaigning, Japan's ship building and pilot training problems could not match the invulnerability of the U.S. Military historian John Keegan called Midway "the most stunning and decisive blow in the history of naval warfare."

GUADALCANAL

Guadalcanal was waged from August 1942 to February 1943. It was, without a doubt, the first major Allied offense of the war. Anemic naval and ground forces augmented by Australian and New Zealand forces gained in six months that clearly overwhelmed the Japanese resistance. Strategically Guadalcanal was the key to overthrowing the Solomon Islands. The rival navies fought several battles. These battles promoting that the carriers were pulled out by both sides as they were too vulnerable to land-based aviation.

BATTLE OF THE PHILIPPINE SEA

In preparation for the Philippines, the navy and Allies started the Gilbert and Marshall Islands campaigns. Enormous training led to a challenging and victorious undertaking.

KAMIKAZE SUICIDE BOMBERS IN WORLD WAR II

Another group makes a stellar mark in history; however, these bombers were a high band of warriors. In 1281 a powerful force invaded Japan. The invaders convinced the Japanese; they called it the "Divine Wind" or kamikaze!

In Japanese culture they followed, a samurai did the principles of Bushido Code. Tenets were: honor, loyalty, courage and self-sacrifice for the emperor imploring disavowal for defeat. During World War II this token was developed to buy time to rebuild their wartime strategy.

In World War II the Japanese Army to Navy had constant argument about the conflict of war: Pearl Harbor and Midway showed a series of out and out beatings of the Japanese military. The Japanese admirals' answer was to reduce training and concentrating of training of principles of kamikaze. Vice Admiral Onishi's plan bears good fruit. The Emperor was satisfied with the tactics and the young pilots.

The main airplane was the "Zero" and was modified to carry a heavy load. This first mission was to Australia carrier, HMAS Australia, was hit killing 30 aboard. The first launch was in October 25, 1944, during the battle for Leyte Gulf near the Philippines. The Japanese success prompted more pilots in the Special Attack Forces, better known as the Kamikaze Suicide Bombers.

The climax of the carrier group was to take the Philippines Sea. Taking control of airfields that would reach Japan, which brought B-29 airplanes within range of Japan. The American logistic effort brought about a complex logistical ninety-day operation which was indicative of the mightiest strength. The army launched a gigantic mission on a more comprehensive American force which the U.S. Navy called the "Great Marines Turkey Shoot," in which many Japanese planes were annihilated.

The Japanese have lost their offensive compatibility and the U.S. has now succeeded in control of Guam, Saipan and Trinidad Islands. The stretch of miles held to the surge of B-29 bombers which raided Japan's homelands. With the Navy aircraft showing other success in air battles they utilized their technological techniques in warfare. This was the longest naval battle in history – surpassed only by the Battle of Leyte Gulf in October 1944.

Japan's strategy during the war was not equal to the U.S. Navy. Nine carriers were for the U.S. 15, 473 compared to 956 airplanes. The list goes on, with the U.S. way ahead of the Japanese. Makoto Ogawa, a Japanese pilot, used a trick and luck strategy that his ballet plan was confusing to the enemy pilots. His aircraft were overloaded with fuel and protective battle armor. The Japanese ships were out of range, but their fuel load would attack the American carriers.

1945 OKINAWA

The last great battle of WW II was Okinawa. The Marines landed in April 1, 1945, to begin an 82-day campaign which no doubt, was the largest land-sea battle in history. It was noted as the bloodiest of the fighting and had the largest number of civilian causalities of the war. This fierce combat plus high American losses led the Navy forces to oppose an invasion of the main islands. A new plan or alternative strategy was selected – use the atomic bomb to bring about surrender of Japan, announced on August 15, 1945, and signed on September 2.

MISTAKES OF WORLD WAR II

The number of mistakes in World War II is mindboggling. The variable beginning to the end of the conflict let many minds to second guess the right or wrong decision. These are couple of blunders through stupidity, ignorance and carelessness. By being blindsided the odds may seem in favor. These are the most favorite and hidden stonewalls to our war.

1. Prime Minister Newville Chamberlin's wrong decision.
    The Prime Minister went to Munich to meet with Adolf Hitler. The reason for this prodigious move was to settle for a peace agreement. Chamberlin met with dignitaries to solve an agreement with all hands. This plan would permit Switzerland in exchange for a hilliest hillside course in exchange for a weightily ease. Finally the arrangement solidified and pleased with the detail. But his integrity was broken and Hitler provided with the courageous acts. Neville Chamberlain has been labeled by history as the worst public figure in the twentieth century.

2. Intelligence Data on December 7, 1941.
    Pearl Harbor was a site where the fleet was located. The Japanese were there but no one realized what was happening behind the scenes. The Japanese fleet was at work planning a technique for dropping a torpedo at a shallow water – to attack the U.S. Fleet. The Japanese Ambassador had been routing a 14-page document which was prepared for the Secretary of State. All along the pictures were taken of the harbor and intelligence commanders were expecting an attack. Commander Admiral Kimmel and the ground troops Lt General Short had no idea of an attack. On alert airplanes were lined up, in rows and sight for an air attack. The

new radar machine was placed on a mountain, detected the wave of Japanese planes which was discounted as a fleet of B-17 coming in from the west coast. And to top it all off, the message was sent to alert the Japanese attack. The communications were tied up and the message was sent by Western Union!

3. Why was Dresden targeted late in the war?
   The major communication network was in Dresden when the focal point was found. Destroying this center could possibly kept the German Army from sending task messages or simply this center was chosen to remain viable because Stalin was not to stray from the agreement earlier in the war.

4. Germany assaults the Union of Soviet Socialist Republics (U.S.S.R.).
   In spite of the Germans' firepower and expertise, their supplies, logistical preparations proved to be short lived. Germany was unable to support a long war and was unable to provide necessary supplies. Operation Barbarossa plays a pivotal role on which side won or lost in the battle of Persia.

5. General Douglas MacArthur returns.
   In December 1941 General MacArthur, the commander of the U.S. Forces in the Pacific, believed his troops could hold off the Japanese. But his troops were weak and with the Japanese moving to the Philippines, he was held in Manila. On December 1941, he withdrew to Bataan Peninsula on the island of Manila. Hit with disease, malaria, and weakened by starvation, they barely maintained their own. In February 1942 President Roosevelt ordered the General to evacuate to Australia. General MacArthur returned to the Philippines on October 20, 1944, with his forces, which wiped out all of the Japanese army and fleet.

6. Codes, Deception and Spies.
   A secret or much more clandestine submarine sailed from Groton, Connecticut and it looked like a German submarine. The submarine made contact with a German submarine, captured the German cipher machine, code named Enigma. The Allies saved two years knowing the code. Also Indian or Navajo code talkers made significant guides by their Marine assaults during 1942 through 1945 until the war ended.

7. Nuclear Bomb – The end was near.

   The last thing the United States had was the nuclear bomb. On August 6, 1945, a B-29, Enola Gay, bombed Hiroshima with the nuclear weapon. The second weapon was dropped on Nagasaki. Without surrendering a B-29 dropped "the fat man" which lay to rest some 15,000 people killed immediately. President Truman explained in a speech, "It was my responsibility as president to force the warlords to come to terms quickly as possible with the minimal loss of lives. They made my final decision. And that final decision was mine alone to make." President Barack Obama would have never, never made that decision looking back on Japan!

CHAPTER 3:

THE KOREAN CONFLICT

BACKGROUND

The war, which ended in 1946, brought peace and tranquility to Americans. It also caused a high level of tension between the United Sates and the Soviet Union. Americans were annoyed and worried about the exportation of communications both at home and abroad. With the Truman Doctrine, Marshall Plan and the Berlin airlift concluded that the spread of communist forced containment especially to Asia. It came to pass that the first major battle waged first in the Korean War.

In 1950 the Peninsula of Korea was divided by the Soviet-backed north and the Americans sided with the south. In August 1945 the Soviet Union attacked North Korea; the United States feared that the North would invade the south, leaving the entire peninsula red. Finally the two countries reached an agreement to divide Korea along the 38th parallel. The Democratic People's Republic led by Kim II Sung ruled the north while nationalist exile Syngman Rhee set up the Republic of Korea (ROK) which re-united their territory under each leader's rule.

War broke out on the 38th parallel on June 25, 1950. The communist led penetrated at several positions along the 38th boundary. The objective was Seoul and had violated the so-called border. United Nations Security Council voted which placed the invasion as a "breach of the peace." President Harry S. Truman committed American forces and named General Douglas MacArthur as Commander of the U.S. forces. The president did not see war but sent American battle forces which amounted to no more than "police action!"

However, the entry of the U.S. signaled a reversal of policy to Korea, Syngman Rhee was behind the U.S.A, but it noted that American troops were withdrawn from South Korea. A sticking point was made by the Secretary of State Dean Acheson, who advocated that the Korean Peninsula lay outside the "defense perimeter" of the U.S.A. This statement that was made was to mean this country would not defend ROK from the communist.

So, the question is asked, why did the United Sates get involved with the Korean Conflict? Enter the Cold War – this grew out of the tense environment that precipitated the decision to intervene. On the eve of the beginning of the conflict, a number of events made President Truman anxious.

Soviet Union exploded an atomic bomb, Soviet action in Turkey and Greece had given rise to the Marshall Plan, which provided funds for aid to war-torn Europe keeping the Soviet from the country. President Truman then ordered the National Security Council to produce a report "NSC68." The council recommends that heavy invasions in military funding which could cause the Soviets to contain at all cost.

Events in Asia caused a great deal of interest in China in 1949. Chairman Mao Tse-tung moved quickly to ally with the Soviet Union with a treaty signed in 1950. Not knowing what he had done, the U.S. president was criticized by the Republicans who claim they had lost China. Secretary of State denounced that the administration endure the communist government of China, which gives them more guns and bullets for those assaults.

The president suffered many and critics, including Republican Senator Joseph McCarthy who began his famous hunt for the communists within the U.S. government. Alger Hiss and others were captured arrested and left others worried about their own communist traits. Therefore, Truman's theory was to quell communism, which has now passed for subversion to conquer and maim other nations and now we have to use armed invasion. The action was part of a bigger plan to involve China which led to Russia. Yet the president had no idea to carry out the hideous attack. The Secretary of State saved the day by giving the Soviet a "graceful exit" and did not carry out a clashing of forces with Russia.

A new military order was affected by Truman's statement. Although the United States took the lead in the Korean action, Truman emphasized that his actions were under the rubric of the United Nations. Regardless, the members of the U.N. were to consider the latest aggression in Korea and America will uphold all rules of war.

George M. Elsey papers had worked with him to solve the World War II issue.

The President met with him and fabricated a draft paper which amplified his second utterance. The proposition was to permit the United Nations to give assistance to South Korea. Secretary of State Acheson assisted the president but this was to no avail. Finally, Truman and other sources later in the day, the United Nation passed his recommendation although a handful of nonconformance of countries did abstain.

KOREA CONFLICT

The U.S. Navy's part in their conflict was to help the United Nations avoid a disaster in the Far East. The invulnerabilities of the U.S. Pacific Fleet and its major element, the Seventh Fleet, permitted President Truman to collaborate his decision to prevent a communist outbreak in Asia. Soon after the North Korean invasion he challenged the Chinese communist forces, the Soviet able and naval forces. He called on a challenge by sending his able fighting forces. Seventh fleet carriers U.S.S. Valley Forge, heavy cruisers U.S.S. Rochester, eight destroyers, and their submarines were extremely busy.

The fleet bombarded the coast as well as the airfields and railyards in Pyongyang, North Korea. Bottom line - the North Korean capital was the nerve center of the emerging military organization.

With the rapid unleash of planes unleashed by Moscow and Beijing, the rapid force of the Seven Fleet proved it was taking effect. Taiwan was in the center eye of attack planes, forces and to end an amphibious assault on this island. The quick deployment of the Far East of U.S. Navy and land-based aircraft influenced Soviet Premier Joseph Stalin to withdraw an earlier pledge of support for Soviet air. For the North Korean attack, however, U.S. submarines and aircraft patrolled between the Soviet and campaign theatre, warning of surprise attacks. By rendezvousing with the carrier forces they operated off the long coast of Chinese in a dexterous role.

MAINTAINING SEA SUPERIORITY

The major objective of the Navy's constant operation was to maintain superiority at sea. Maybe by coincident at no time did the North Korea or Soviet vision use the sea air to support the communists in Korea. This move also helped MacArthur's Far East Command slow down the 1950 ground offensive. This aggressive setup of a beachhead permitted a build up for a counteroffensive.

One of the Navy's first actions was to destroy small vessels. The enemy propelled the attacks by using a bold, strategic attempt to seize Pusan by landing troops near the port. A North Korean victory could leave doomed the effort to set foot in South Korea. But, those 600 troops never landed. The Fleet's mobility countered the seas and General MacArthur plus United Nations turned the tide. In mid-September, the Command of the Seventh Fleet Task Force, Vice Admiral Arthur D. Struble leads a moving force of 200 planes and other ships in a surprise bombardment of the port of Inchon. Koreans were toast.

The name operation Chromite consisted of the Maine 1st and 5th regiments of the Marine 1st Division led the courageous attack. Many of the Allies doubted the major amphibious task at Inchon at high tide. At low tide many ships were under the threat of being stuck in the mud. The assault commenced on September 12 at 8:33 a.m. by shelling by cruisers, bombardment of aircraft and naval fire by support ships. These objectives were secured by the morning hours of September 16.

McArthur helped for another Inchon landing but the amphibious force was stymied with Soviet-supplied mines which blocked the approach to Wonsan. This setback was delivered to the mine sweeper ships as several were sunk. Despite the horrendous difficulties, the Task Force 95 conquered the mine issue and led to a loss-free sea channel to Chinnampo, the port serving the loss of Pyongyang. All in all, the troops found it outnumbered which containing the Marine 1st Division and the Army 3rd and seventh Infantry divisions. Thus, these fighting men were evacuated by sea from the eastern port of Hungnam and Wonsan.

On December 10, 1950 the withdrawal began when Task Force 90 took on elements of Marines which finished masterful fighting from chosen carriers. Philippine Sea, Valley Forge, Princeton, and Leyte Gulf plus other escort cruisers provided 1700 sorties during one week of combat. In the meantime, the battleship Missouri, cruisers St. Paul and Rochester including a massive group of destroyers provided a ring of fire around the Allied troops. More than 23,000 rounds of shells fell over Chinese and North Korean forces – herded against the United Nations perimeter. By Christmas Eve, the Navy seals, destroyed the port facilities at Hungnam. The Navy had withdrawn 105,000 troops and thousands others with 17,500 vehicles. Clearly, the Navy had control of the sea, gave the X-Corps will live and fight another day!

The navies of the United Nations also maintained a naval blockade of North Korean coastlines. This created the enemy from using the sea and allowed Allies to move freely. Strategically, this enabled submarines to enter and to permit underwater demolition teams (UDTs) to land on many costal islands. The elite units destroyed enemy railroads, highway bridges, and supply depots. While the harassment was ongoing, the guerillas went onshore for long periods of time behind enemy lines. Starting February 16, 1951, this Allied fleet pushed back, hung on and pushed back to North Korea 80,000 troops!

Sea control was of prime importance during the last two years of this war. The most important scenario was to make their negotiating position by having cease-fire talks at Panmunjom. Leaving the best for last, the enemy was forced to sign the Armistice Treaty ending the Korean War on July 27, 1953.

WHAT WENT WRONG IN THE KOREAN WAR

General Douglas MacArthur was the American general who commanded the Southern Pacific in World War II. President Truman, president of the United States (POTUS), appointed him as Commander of the United Nations forces in 1950 – 1953 in the Korean War. Controversy arose when the General MacArthur and President Truman had a serious spat.

President Truman and General MacArthur decided on a new set of war criteria. It was to liberate the north from the hated Communist. With continued success, the President did not want a war which would lead to Soviet aggression in Europe. Apparently General MacArthur thought it was an appeasement which was an unacceptable way of dealing with the Communist regime. Finally with letters flying from President Truman, General MacArthur wrote "…no substitute for victory…" against Communism. For Truman, this letter was the last straw. On April 11, 1951, he fired the general for insubordination!

CHAPTER 4:

THE COLD WAR

In 1945 during World War II the submarine was making a mockery of the U.S. Navy. In the Pacific Ocean sound channels into the sea detected U.S. Navy airplanes shot down by enemy Japanese airplanes or shot by gunfire from battleships or various destroyers. By equating these crashes of U.S. aircraft many of these pilots were rescued by Navy PBY-5 aircraft. This threat, however, was stymied by the last of information consuming oceanographic and acoustic conditions. It became obvious that the German Navy had a better idea, Atlantic or Pacific, on the oceans on either side of the United States. Since the close of the war, the navy conducted an intensive program of oceanographic surveys designed to give data on currents, temperature, salinity and other factors which comprise the oceanic background and, therefore, affect the transmission of sound in sea water. The U.S. Navy is resolved never again to be behind no one in the knowledge of this vital area.

The program requires oceanographic and acoustic surveys worldwide in all avenues of the areas. Many ships may be if not available to collect this data dedicated to the mission on a consistent priority. By ships, this is a process. With rapid techniques we plus various electronics, have made it possible to connect this source of data by means of shore stations. Therefore, at least they are U.S. Naval facilities.

The headquarters of evaluation counters of Naval Facilitates will not act as a repository of data received by means of high speed communications. This will permit users to use the data requested. Several of the data will be provided to the Fleet ASW (anti-submarine warfare). Data Analysis Program for post recognition of the overall picture for accurate operation. Actual oceanographic information is a real time factor to the Fleet Commander. This is a vital factor in solving a successful ASW operation. Alas, the Oceanographic System Commander's report to their respective Fleet Commander.

So, the 1950s and the 1960s gave both of development and growth of surveillance, originally the Sound Surveillance System (SOSUS). With the 1970s came technology upgrades in both shore and in underwater devices. This more aptly put training for new cable ships, super NAVFACs and the follow on the Towed Array Sensor System (TASS), the Surveillance Towed Array Sensor System (SURTASS). In the 1980s increased reliability plus engineering phenomena in underwater systems, arrival of the first SURTASS ships, delivering of the cable ship USNS Zeus and the end of the Cold War. The 1990s, where we are today! Let's find out.

In 1949 the Navy decided to explore passive sonar in its ASW inventory. Project Hartwell under Massachusetts Institute of Technology (MIT) leadership initiated a long range project for submarines defense. The result of the committee was that the answer is to the submarine diesel snorkeling problems. The Hartwell Committee recommended $10 million dollars that would be applied to an efficacious long range acoustic detection system sensor using a bottom array. In 1951 a 6-element test array was installed at Eleuthera in the Bahamas. This highly classified project was called Project Jezebel.

In 1952 six more sets of lofar stations were deployed in the North Atlantic basin with a Top Secret letter. The classified name was SOSUS and increased the number of stations to nine. Eleuthera put in a 40 element array and Bahamas was installed also. In 1954 ten additional stations, three Atlantic, six Pacific and one Hawaii, were authorized. Key West was installed with NAVFAC Ramey, Puerto Rico, followed by NAVFAC Grand Turk and San Salvador.

In 1958 the Commander, Oceanographic System was established. Many NAVFACs were opened particularity NAVFAC Argentia, Newfoundland was opened in 1959. In June 26, 1962, the first detection of a Soviet submarine was made by an Oceanographic station. One July 6 NAVFAC Barbados made the first detection of a Russian nuclear submarine. In 1964 the Command, Oceanographic System was established. The program was delegated to OP-95, the Director of ASW Programs under VADM Charles B. Martell. NAVFAC Keflavik, Iceland was installed and was to deploy one year. SOSUS was deployed to the Norwegian Sea.

This was the beginning of a SOSUS network that detected Soviets both east, west of the United States and deployed sites; it gave a heads up to contact heading south protecting the Greenland-Iceland-United Kingdom (GUIK) gap. With the phenomenal senses of the NAVFAC, the detection of the Soviet submarine falls to the airplane. Pending World War II, the P2V was built by Lockheed, had the APS-20 radar and P2V-5 had installed the Magnetic Anomaly Detection (MAD) which was an extension to the tail of the aircraft. More important was the AN/ASA13 "sniffer" which was a Foxtrot submarine east of Cuba in 1963. Sonar buoys came from the war and were dropped to detect submarines. The main feature was the gear known as "Jezebel." By dropping sound buoys the signal is sent to the AQA-3 or AQA-4, which is manned by an operator. On these lines or grams the submarine is detected. Twelve squadrons on the east coast and similar number were deployed trying to detect submarines. They deployed every ten months and the missions expanded when they were hunting submarines with the help of the Oceanographic System.

In 1962 October the President of the United States out-trumped the Soviet Union leader. This led to a blockade in the Atlantic Ocean of U.S. vs. the Russian fleet. U.S. ships, submarines, P-3 Orion, and the SOSUS network were at full alert! Due to differing opinions relating to Communism, the two argumentative superpowers, engaged in rivalry which threatened the world – Mutual Assured Destruction. Both armed with nuclear weapons, they fought only through minor contacts and threats. The situation fluctuated between the years, but increased to a new height to its peak during the late 1960s. Throughout this period the threat of nuclear war existed especially during the fourteen days of the Cuban Missile Crisis. The shortest appearance of Cuban Missiles halted resolutions between U.S. and the U.S.S.R, principally due to trust – this without a doubt was the summit of tension during the Cold War.

In 1991 President Ronald Reagan tore down the wall which signified the end of the Cold War.

Believe it or not the Cold War continues!

CHAPTER 5:

THE VIETNAM WAR

INTRODUCTION

The 1954 – 1975 was a prolonged conflict that pitted the Communist forces of North Vietnam and its allies in South Vietnam, often known as the Vietcong, against the government of South Vietnam with its primary ally, the United States. The "American War" was called the "War Against the Americas to Save the Nation." This war was part of a larger engagement and is an act of the Cold War between the USA and the Soviet Union.

At the heart of the battle was the desire of North Vietnam which had defeated the French colonial management of Vietnam in 1954. This rational would unify into a single communist state modeled after those of the Soviet Union and China. On the other hand, South Vietnam liked to pressure their government closely with the West. Beginning in 1950, small numbers of military advisors and increasing slowly in manpower in 1961. Active combat units were brought in 1965. 500,000 troops were eventually assigned. Meanwhile, the Soviets and China poured armies and supplies, with many advisors into the North to induce the secret plans to the North Vietnam. The cost and the casualties were too much for the United States to bear. Eventually the U.S. combat troops were withdrawn in 1973. In 1975 South Vietnam fell to a large scale invasion of the North.

Vietnam emerged from the war as a potent military power. Large parts of this country were marred by bombs, land mines, and defoliation from Agent Orange.

A mass of people in 1975 and the boat people in 1978 was due to the loyal people of South Vietnam.

FRENCH RULE ENDED, VIETNAM DIVIDED

The Vietnam War was devised in the broader wars of Indochina in the 1940s and 1950s. These outbreaks obscured where nationalist groups, Ho Chi Minh's Vietnam were inspired by Chinese and Soviet communism. The French Indochina War began in 1946 and carried on for eight years with France's effort being supplied by the United States. With the blow of losing to Viet Minh at the Battle of Dien Bien Phu in May 1954, the French came to the end of battle in Indochina.

This battle yielded the Geneva Conference to produce Geneva Accords which established the 17th parallel, latitude 17 degrees west, as the demarcation line separating the forces of the French and Vietnam. North was the Democratic Republic of Vietnam which carried out an eight-year strife with the French. The North was characteristic of the workers Party led by Ho Chi Minh, in Hanoi, the capital. In the South, the capital is Saigon. Within 300 days a Demilitarized Military Zone (DMZ), which caused the back and forth movement of the 17th parallel line. The nationwide election would be held on 1956, once the civilians decided which side –north or south they preferred.

Pledging the de facto portion of the 17 degree parallel appears to be incapable of avoiding spreading communism in Asia. Dwight D. Eisenhower instituted a crash program to ensure that the state of South Vietnam was acknowledged. The Saigon Military Mission was programmed to provide under the command of U.S. Air Force Colonel Edward Lansdale. Vietnam was expecting disarray of political means but somehow retained their grasp with respect to their leader Ngo Dinh Diem. His power was just and fought to stay above the 17 degree parallel.

Support of the U.S. Army, who kept retained in all types of weapons, was diligent in mounting the DMZ time. The Central Intelligence Agency (CIA) made Diem angry with domestic opposition, and had agencies help him to regain his economy and help him resettle the Chinese and of Russian refugees, 900,000 fleeing to South Vietnam.

Diem has consolidated his power in the south. He arrested those who confessed their communist favors. In October 1955 Diem called for a referendum in the south. The north, however, were not ready to commence a war-like posture and were unable to induce the Chinese or Russia allies to act.

The Diem regime had surprised the Washington D.C. officials and military economic aid poured into South Vietnam. Thus the American military and police advisors began training and thus equipping Diem's army – all in all, the problems were in the administrative branch, which refused to delegate authority. Ngo Dinh Nhu, his brother, controlled a vast system of extortion, payoffs, which gave a large invasion of piddling through a secret system which was called the Can Lao. This network sparked the government officials, military units, schools, newspapers, to mention a few. Police and other secret units were engaged in all types of bribery. Diem himself were acting as officials, northern, and Roman Catholics found themselves further hostile to that of the local inhabitants.

Diem's challenge towards the Communist faction against party organizers in the countryside in 1955 resulted in the arrest of thousands in the temporary not organized in the communist infrastructure. By 1957 the Viet Cong (VC) had begun a program of level assassinations among government officials commencing 1959, bands of VC were occasionally engaged in South Vietnam in violent clashes.

By this time, the main body of the Vietnamese party meeting in Hanoi, North Vietnam ordered a plan calling for the use of armed forces to inflict destruction to the Diem government! Southerners that were specifically trained above the DMZ were quickly brought back into South Vietnam with weapons. A war has begun!

The army called the ARUN, or the Republic of Vietnam, was in many ways not able to withstand the Viet Cong. The often pathetic higher ranking officers were corrupt. The penetrations by the Cong of Navy officers ran through the ranks all the way to the senior headquarters. Heavy with its American-style equipment, the ARUN centered on road type force not the VC units in swamps or downright jungles. The language was the problem – Vietnamese. This was the major blunder!

In 1960 the communists in the south founded the National Liberation Front (NLF), which served the political arm of the Viet Cong, which abhorred these who wanted an end to the Diem regime. This regular army called the main force, was much smaller than threat of Diem's militia. The Guerilla units formed from the PLA made up a recruiting agency in which workers lived at houses and worked in normal work habits during the day. These men were better equipped, full-time soldiers, in remote jungle or swamps, including mountainous area. When these guerillas achieved their goals, the full-time forces might draft several units into a special mission.

THE U.S. ROLE GROWS

By the middle of 1960 it was apparent that South Vietnam was in serious trouble since 1959. VC had numerous ambushes or attacks, which had struck ARUN. It took some time to realize that Saigon and Washington D.C. know how the VC was powerful. Four VC companies attacked and had overrun the ARUN headquarters near Saigon January 1960. It took that task for the U.S. to plan for U.S. aid to Diem! A futile search was begun to thwart antagonistic VC and move him back to North Vietnam.

To the new administration President John F. Kennedy represented a new challenge – the Vietcong army superiority over Diem. Another act of challenge is the "War of National Liberation" which helped the spread of communist powers to Asia and Africa. The president countered by "counter-insurgency" against its ally or its guerrilla warfare. President Kennedy also accepted the domino theory, which closes out the successor of one country invalidates another. "The cornerstone of the free world in Southern Asia," said President Kennedy would cement by allies and adversaries, would provide the U.S. determination to meet the communist expansion in the Third World.

The success seemed urgently needed as the VC continued to pour south. U.S. intelligence estimated in 1960 4,000 men inflicted from the north – 1962 the total has risen to 12,000! Of the group some were South Vietnam regrouped, and more than half were of the Communist Party! Hardened and elite, they provided a framework of PLAF. Hanoi leaders began to arm and fire powers in steel huddle motor junks through South Vietnam, but through Laos eventually a network of jungle tracks known to all as the Ho Chi Minh Trail. Most of the warfare items were gained by American rifles and numerous items that were captured from Saigon forces. Another way war, simply sold to the enemy by corrupt officers of Diem armed forces!

As foretold brought services problems to Vietnam, President Kennedy appointed Walt Rostow and Maxwell Taylor to assess the conditions. All in all, the two agreed that the South Vietnam government was giving the war away!

Of the proposal, they recommended helicopters and armored personnel carriers with a plan to place the American advisers in the agencies of South Vietnam. They also endorsed a limited number of U.S. troops, which the Joint Chiefs of Staff wanted immediately. So, therefore, a new four star general was established – Commander U.S. Military Assistant Commander Vietnam (USMACV).

THE CONFLICT DEEPENS

Escalated by the plus of American troops, the offensive started. The strategic Hamlet program undertook a strong security program. Meanwhile, the Vietcong soon became used to the American weapons of the ARUN. The apparent realization that ARUN leadership was weak. This was noted by the surrounding of the ARUN in AP back in the Mekong Delta. The aggressive forces of American troops were labeled as serious deficiencies in the warfare fight.

Enter Madam Nhu – North Vietnam's Nhu's wife, she used Roman Catholics social cases which ridiculed the country's Buddhist majority. Strikes and demonstrations by Buddhists in Saigon and the Hue were met with violence by the army and Nhu's security forces which led to many arrests.

AIRCRAFT CARRIER U.S.S. ORISKANY CV-35

The entry into the conflict was inevitable as one of the carriers was called to assist the struggle. The U.S.S. Oriskany, fresh with an overhaul in 1964, set sail for Vietnam in 1965. She was carrying an air wing consisting of F-8A Cruisers and Douglas A-4D Sky Hawks. Oriskany began chasing targets as part of "Reputation Rolling Thunder." Over the next several months, she used Yankee or Dixie Station attacking targets. Flying over 12,000 missions she received the Naval Unit Commendation.

Returning to San Diego in 1965, she had an additional overhaul and began streaming back to Vietnam. A massive fire caused by air mishandled force killed 43 men and injured 38 sailors. She sailed back to the Philippines where the injured men recovered. The carrier sailed to San Francisco for repairs.

U.S.S. Oriskany – CV-34 back to Vietnam repaired, she was surviving as the flagship of Carrier Division 9. She assumed Yankee Station, one of Oriskany's pilots. LCDR John McCain was shot down over North Vietnam. A future senator, and presidential candidate and released five years later, he and several others were unleashed. Oriskany completed another overhaul and it arrived on station in 1964. Yankee Station was a prime target for the Ho Chi Minh Trail: Operation Steel Tiger was a threat to the missile attack by North Vietnam. In November Oriskany returned to Alameda for dry dock where it handled the LTV A-7 Corsair II attack aircraft.

In 1970 the carrier was docked on station delivering bombs on the Ho Chi Minh Trail, additionally she participated in the "Son Tay rescue" mission as she entered the sixth tour of Vietnam. The Soviet TU-95 Bear aircraft overflew the carrier as well as Navy fighters shadowed the bombers as they in the area.

Launching strikes and destroying MIG airplanes they continued many airstrikes. In January 27, 1973, the final Paris Peace Accords were signed.

Back on the land struggle, the President went to Johnson. He had General Westmoreland recommending adding more troops and different tactics which were analyzed and thrown them in the garbage can! President Johnson did not want a declaration of war, the National Guard or military rescuers were called in but this was part of a mobilization plan. General Westmoreland led the air war and charged assignments in the Army. In Saigon, the frequent recurrences of political instability ceased where a force general took command as head of state and responsible for the air force with Nguyen Cao Ky prime minister.

The South Vietnamese forces became second hand with the U.S. forces flooded the south. Air fields and deep water piers came into fruition. General Westmoreland's plan was to take the battle to North Vietnam. He surprised that this effort took to the jungles and mountains. Because General Westmoreland's strategy was based on attrition, in other words, the body count! A program for the "Pacification and Long Term Development of Vietnam" (PROVN) authored by a U.S. Army Chief of Staff prioritized the flaw of General Westmoreland. He documented the security and ineffective rural population and would not work as a good counterinsurgency strategy. PROVW was not selected by commanders, yet the impress is overwhelming—firepower or "seek and destroy" missions were a real hit in the soldier war.

In the northern areas large operations such as Cedar Falls and Junction City were mounted by helicopters, planes or fighter bombers, which deviated communist supplies and troops. Once their territory was won, the Vietcong regrouped and came back in their battle field. The Vietcong used dense forest to conceal movement of supply lines. The U.S. Air Force used a herbicide code named "Agent Orange" along the Vietnamese border, Laos and Cambodia, and along waterways. The land was wiped clan of vegetation, leaving thousands of people with toxic chemicals, which could lead to death.

Along the DMZ, the Americans planted numerous bases all along the border. Warning devices, mines and other killing agents, namely infrared detection system rated in the highest number of casualties. The North Vietnamese artfully favored its mark during this stalemate. The battles continued through 1966. Bombings had better effect during the conflict. North Vietnam continued to field airplanes and the red loss more aircraft during the conflict.

The turning point of the war, which were, by the end of 1967 there were 540,000 soldiers with 302,000 called up raising the total to an aggregate of 72,000 troops. South Vietnam won 37 of 45 engagements, General Westmoreland because the *Time* magazine Man of the year and the response that U.S. and its allies were closing the gap in Vietnam.

The Tet Offensive shocked all hands! Even Walter Cronkite returned to what has transpired! White and blacked reared its ugly head. Even white troops wore black arm bands when they went on patrol. In March 1968, the My Lai massacre took place with over 100 women and children who lost their lives. Many antiwar protesters blamed the men who translated to nurses, who were told not to wear their uniforms in the U.S.A.

Next it becomes President Richard Nixon's war followed by the "Vietnamization," during which South Vietnam began to take over the responsibility of the war. Security was improving as the American troops started sending troops home. President Nixon ordered Haiphong harbor to be mined in North Vietnam. President Nixon ordered intensified bombing of North Vietnam. After two weeks of intensive strategic, bombing its explosives ruined the North's defenses. On January 27, 1973, peace accords were signed by the U.S. and the North Vietnamese.

MISTAKES THE VIETNAM CONFLICT MADE

1. The mistakes are overburdening! North and South Vietnam were plagues with mistakes which only prolonged the blood flow. Prominent were the stakes that errored President Nixon. He should have given South Vietnam the responsibility to take control of the war. It never happened.

2. The Ho Chi Minh Trail was a disaster responsibility of these conflicts. Thousands of supplies went down the road and then at daylight they were not visible to the Americans and the South Vietnamese.

3. Special P-2 Neptune aircrafts were sent to track and report surveillance based on listening devices dropped at night. They were defenseless while the majority of the squadron was shot down.

4. Rolling Thunder was used as an asset to penetrate or demoralize the jungle, leaving a fertile area with nothing left but dirt. There must have been another option for this bombing. This bombing was called Agent Orange. Any U.S., anybody that was near the area, the wind blowing toward you,

can contact this deadly substance. The Veterans administration has many Agent Orange cases which they treat but normally they pass away.

5. The Tet Offensive brought hate among the Armed Forces. The crowds in the United States were dismayed. Anti-protesters or antiwar protesters blamed the men and women serving in Vietnam. They spit, roughly shouting, and threw rocks at them when they came home.

6. The lingering legacies of war in the media cost us the war. The burning of a monk, living of others pointing a gun at the head of a Vietcong prisoner, or a naked young girl running after an American napalm strike. These all keep deep down in the mind of people like us, the American mindset!

Fonda Speaks To Vietnam Veterans At Anti-War Rally

Actress And Anti-War Activist Jane Fonda Speaks to a crowd of Vietnam Veterans as Activist and former Vietnam Vet John Kerry (LEFT) listens and prepares to speak next concerning the war in Vietnam (AP Photo)

CHAPTER 6:

THE GULF WAR

This war was the most efficient effort of wartime in American history. Undoubtedly, the loss of lives was low, but the technology and U.S. doctrine offered a potent force applied to world power. These problems will be answered when the conflict is terminated:

a. As a renewed look at Iraq and how they were prompted to attack southward.

b. Kuwait – a case of having a conquest of a small nation.

c. Saudi Arabia was afraid more or less of Saddam Hussein's war – like posture so it had enough guts to stimulate U.S. interest.

d. The U.S.A. accepted this challenge and played a commanding role by opposing Iraq.

e. It took some time, but the coalition of forces built up sufficient manpower to overturn the Iran/Iraq war.

f. Both the air war and the ground war were a savage blow, which led to a humbling victory. Both the ground/air war only lasted for four days. What happened, what outlasted the victories – all factors will be addressed after the engagement.

FACTORS THAT LED TO IRAQ INVADING KUWAIT

Iraq Gulf War began with the term "Nation of Iraq." Once a country of Ottoman Empire and several other countries to add, she became a totalitarian state with Saddam Hussein became president in 1979. The Kurds yearned for independence and in the south, the Shiites looked to Iran. The state and the army grew to consume most of the gross national product (GNP). Today, 35 percent of every dollar earned, the military takes.

Saddam's expansion of the military apparatus was fighting because his investments in nuclear, chemical and biological weapons. Corresponding declining systems even prompted an attack by Israel to set back his weapons with an attack in 1981. Saddam attempted to gain domination over the Persian Gulf region, when in the 1980s, when he fought a bitter Iran.

As a result of a battle with Iran, the Iraqi Military became the overpowering force in the area. Iraq borrowed oil heavily from its many neighbors. This debt coupled with lending investments brought on a 40 percent inflation rate and a stagnant standard of living.

Although Iraq has oil reserves of her own, revenue could not meet her creditors. This problem was realized in 1990 when Kuwait and other participates began to lower oil prices, bringing production below agreed upon levels. To make matters worse Iraq suspected Kuwaitis were dueling diagonally from the border to keep Iraq oil reserves.

Thus Saddam Hussein was now in deep shit! It was more difficult for Hussein to maintain his military command. He seemed to think there was only one way to extend his angry; he sought a solution involving a foreign adventure.

THE GULF WAR – KUWAIT

Saddam Hussein found himself in a predicament and a quick turnover of Kuwait seems like a quick solution to his problem. Kuwait was a small country that had been in the confines of the Ottoman Empire. When this country had been gained independence, its borders had been set in an arbitrary manner. Its borders are not readily defensible and its population is not unified. This country was ruled by an Emir of the al Sabah family.

Most of the countries in the Persian Gulf region are dependent on the oil industry. All in all the population was small, thereby its military was below the average. Saddam in Iraq comparing bottom falling oil prices, Kuwait unknowing gave the six signs of leaving Iraq was success fueling the Iran/Iraq war. Iraq claimed the entire region from the "Iranian steamroller in 1980s and deserved excellent consideration!"

July of 1990 Saddam had built up his military forces near the border of Kuwait. At 1:00 a.m. August 1, the Iraq divisions rolled over the border. Resistance was nearly non-existent as they reached the outskirts of the capital, Kuwait City. This was attained only four and a half hours later. The frontal attack was achieved by an airborne Special Forces division assault on Kuwait City alone.

Saddam pronounced his accomplishment by crushing Kuwait, added to the power of his forces, and waited to see whether the world would do anything about his fait accompli!

THE SAUDI INVASION

The Middle East is a region of interlaced policies evolving family ties, rulers, religious strife, and human personalities. This unstable area, the entire world was aghast with the Iraq invasion of Kuwait. This country was part of Iraq and it was a power play by Saddam to take the world's producing oil fields. Incidentally, Saddam collectively had 20% of the overall oil reserves.

The Republic Guard had secured all the cross points and intersections as it moved to the Kuwait and Saudi border. It was a new buildup of forces which countered the elite troops in the region. Intelligence forces warned that more combat divisions were moving to Kuwait, Saudi Arabia saw the signs of imminent danger and possible takeover.

King Fahd of Saudi Arabia was advised of the dangers of the turn of events. He requested President Bush help the dismal predicament! The President promptly ordered ground and air forces as U.S. Navy ships were sent to this area. Thus began "Desert Storm" to Saudi Arabia to protect this country from Saddam.

U.S. INTEREST IN THE GULF WAR

Saddam Hussein's moves well in conflict should but the strategist had different ideas that Saudi Arabia was not to be attacked or otherwise stormed over in any way and Iraq massive force. Having obliterated Kuwait, Saddam had 20% of the world's oil and Saudi Arabia 26% of the oil reserves, boy, what could he do with this.

Besides the economic factors controlling American lives, there were influences that control our own destiny. In its invasion of Kuwait, many atrocities were found on those captured people. This aligned from torture, executions, to blatant rape. Many Americans thought that this could lead to be accelerated if Saddam invaded Saudi Arabia.

Weapons of Mass Destruction were weighing in across the Iraq nation. The Central Intelligence Agency and other intelligent agents thought Iraq was on the steps of developing a nuclear as well as a biological warfare as well. No doubt they had chemical warehouses that stored chemical agents. Iraq was very bold about their showing their display and the obvious threat of the Kurdish independence movement.

All too soon the economic sanctions failed to keep Saddam from courting evil tactics, but there pursued him from developing weapons of mass destruction. All these problem areas failed: they could not keep out of Kuwait. Military force was the verdict!

BUILD-UP OF FORCES

Saddam Hussein's move into Iraq was so alarming that it galvanized most of the nations in the region that was to help Saudi Arabia to oppose the Iraq build up. The United Nations looked for support in future war. A final determination of the United Nations was to condemn Iraq and demand immediate removal of all forces from Kuwait.

General Norman "Stormin'" Schwarzkopf was sent by President Bush to take command of U.S. forces and a de facto commune of forces sent to the region. Sent to the General was the election force of XVIII Airborne Corp (24 Mechanized Infantry Division, 101 Airborne Division, and the 82nd Airborne Division). The Marine 1st Division was sent in which, over 500,000 personnel were sent. Other allies: Britain, France, Egypt and Syria which took over international role, with the United States in command.

The engagement happened so rapidly that Schwarzkopf wondered if Iraq invaded without a proper strategic defense. The think tank offered the scenario that if Saddam had ordered his troops to attack Saudi with the timeframe of a few days after attacking Kuwait, these would be any doubt he would be rolling into Riyadh! Saddam halted but he no knows the time has come there to "test the metal" of combined forces!

On January 30, 1991, the Iraq 15th Mechanized Infantry Brigade attacked Al-Khafji, a small town in Saudi Arabia. This encounter was rapidly repelled leaving clear Saddam would only be happy when Saddam took Kuwait. Desert Shield in 1991 brought Colin Powell after he advised the Joint Chiefs of Staff, that they were determined to take the war to Iraq.

AIR WAR – OPERATION DESERT STORM

The name of the game is air superiority! This technique gives the aggressor to indiscriminately destroying enemy targets, stop enemy supply lines, recon, and upset the ability that the adversary can't do the things himself. On January 16, 1991, the air campaign commenced after the U.N. deadline for Iraqi withdrawal from Kuwait. The air superiority took charge by destroying radar installations, by helicopters; Baghdad was by eliminated command and control centers, F-11s and other aircraft annihilated hangers and air bases. U.S. Navy employed Tomahawk missiles and Navy bombers wreaked utter havoc on all aspects of Iraq air. Incidentally, the air was involved by Saudi, British, French, Italy and various Arab Air Forces.

The Allied air power literally blew away all targets that Iraq went to psychological means that used human hostages as shields for targets. Secondly, they placed their aircraft in hold placed knowing that the allies would be reluctant to attack ("collateral damage").

In an effort to highlight the air war, two F-1 Mirage fighters loaded with incendiary bombs with two M16-23s as backups, were intercepted by the U.S. AWACs. Two Royal Saudi F-15 aircraft were sent to intercept. When the F-15s gained contact, the M16s hightailed as one Saudi pilot shot down both Iraq aircraft! This made the cork come out of the bottle as the Iraqi flew their jets to Iran in hopes they would claim air superiority again. Iran did not return their aircraft!

With the air power neutralized the Allied air forces continued to strike with repeated blows in Kuwait and Southern Iraq. Field bombs, cluster bombs, and armor-piercing guided bombs were the killers. B-52 bombers were wiping out entire regiments, brigades and divisions. By late February the coalition was ready to proceed with the ground attack.

THE GROUND WAR – OPERATION DESERT STORM

Argument over the ground versus air comparing was the topic of today. The air assault was overwhelming when defeating the Iranians in Kuwait. It was known as "the great prisoner round-up." On February 24, 1991, the Marines started their push that thrust into the Iraq forces holding Kuwait. The Saudi and Muslim forces attacked Kuwait along the coastline. The 18th Airborne Corps plus the French 6th Armored Division with high speed rushed into Iraq from the left. Other attacks were mounted by U.S VII troops joined by British 7th Armored Division.

General Schwarzkopf's strategy relied heavily on a flanking maneuver. He placed the Allied Forces to combat front line troops while they were encircled on the left. This move was highly effective by cutting lines of supply by denying on escape route. Based in Kuwait and being harassed by the Allies, the Iraqis had only one major avenue to take. They were bombarded, stranded; and were left with burning remains of their elite forces. Motion pictures were flashed across the United States as they were called "Highway of Death." As the collation forces seals the last cubby hole of retreat, Allied leaders including the President thought the last had been won. On February 28 President Bush ordered completion of this war.

MISTAKES OF THE GULF WAR

1. Many questions were still being asked – "Was U.S. involvement justified?" "Did the coalition soldiers end too soon?" The agreements permitted Saddam Hussein to withdraw their units intact. He remained in power as the Iraqi war element was quickly dismantled.

2. More that considering was to do in the Middle East. The agreement fell in three areas:

    a. Many felt it would be unwise to establish a buffer between Iran and Arabia.

    b. Saddam was perceived as a hero by many in the Middle East, mainly Palestinians and Jordanians, and

    c. There is a certain unique brotherhood that Arabs acknowledge for one another.

3. Saddam would surely cause trouble down the road by violating peace statues and continuing work on weapons of mass destruction.

4. Outstanding among Lee, and other stalwarts, General Schwarzkopf's campaign was, without a doubt, a brilliance unsurpassed! His offensive charge was swift and decisive. He received all of every resource available at his disposal.

5. In the end, there was a popular war that favored the Western world. It confirmed the air and ground war that was superior and left armed conflict never prevails in nations that are determined to see freedom abound!

CHAPTER 7:

AFGANISTAN WAR

The Afghanistan war began its conflict beginning in 2001 that was promoted by September 11 attacks which involved their accounts.

Phase one – defeating the Taliban, the ultra-conservative or a political religious faction that ruled Afghanistan, provided sanctuary for Al-Qaeda who was responsible for the September 11, 2001 attack. Secondly, from 2002 through 2008 was marked by the U.S. defeating Taliban on the battlefield and rebuilding of the Afghan state. The third phase was to turn to counter-insurgency agency doctrine 2008 and accelerated with President Barrack Obama's decision to increase U.S. troops in Afghanistan. The larger force was to protect the population from Taliban attacks while supporting integrating those insurgents into Afghan society.

Beginning in 2011 all security problems would be handed over to Afghan military and the police force. This idea did not succeed; the number of attacks on people as well as military attacks and police were attacked sufficient but were ill-prepared to hold off the Taliban.

By December 2014, the United States North Atlantic Treaty Organization (NATO) forces had spent 13 years of supporting Afghanistan – the longest engagement endured by the United States!

PRELUDE TO THE SEPTEMBER ATTACKS

Two decades had been battled over Afghanistan when U. S. and Britain invaded in 2001. Russian tanks motored across the Amu Darya River to restore sanity following a coup that brought power to a joint Marxist-Leninist power group. The Russian appearance lit the powder keg of rebellion by Islamist soldiers which opened the door to covert backing from Pakistan. At this time the U.S. and Saudi Arabia joined hands to stave off their fight against the foreign advocates! These radicals led the Russians to leave early over ten years in the vivid number of military warriors of war knows as the mujahedeen. They chased the Russian armada out of the government and then turning their pieces against each other.

In 1996 the Taliban seized Kabul, and installed a severe interpretation of Islamic law which forbade female education, allowed severing of hands, or even execution possible as punishment for petty crimes. That Al-Qaeda leader Osama bin Laden was welcomed to Afghanistan over to set forth his organization's main network. Taliban gained control of over 90% of the Afghan territory and September 9 Al-Qaeda hatchet men killed former leader Ahmad Shah Massoud who had failed to get U.S. help for his total work done to achieve a particular end.

The horrific September 11, 2001, brought memories of Afghanistan. The plot has been constructed by Al-Qaeda in the same country. President George W. Bush was to unite for a common end around a strategy by ousting Al-Qaeda. Others planned an attack on Iraq, including alluring plans for Saddam Hussein. President Bush demanded that the Taliban "deliver to the United States all leaders of Al-Qaeda who reside in you providence." When Omar repudiated, U.S. intelligence began implementing a war plan.

A campaign in Afghanistan erupted covertly on September 26 with the Central Intelligence Agency (CIA) arriving in the country and working with an anti-Taliban alliance, thus a project was generated to overthrow the regime. U.S. officials thought they would partake with the Afghans thereby avoid sufficient forces but not to hinder broad based occupation of Afghanistan. The Pentagon was almost concerned that their implementation of more forces would precipitate the same similar occurrence that the Soviets tried two decades ago. The United States had lost Massoud but with a collection including Tajik leader Mohammed Fahim and Abdul Rashid Dostum who was an Uzbek. The American teamed with anti-Taliban Pashtuns, a little known leader to wit, Hamid Karzai.

The CIA team was amplified by U.S. and British special forces and together they provided arms and associated items to the Afghans' air attack was with targeting which offered pounding of Taliban forces giving the operation Enduring Freedom a welcome arrival. Northern Alliance overtook several towns which by the other hand overtook towns held by Taliban. Forces worked with harmony but turned their back on U.S. forces when they marched into Kabul as the opponent retreated without even a mummer of firepower!

Kandahar was the Taliban home; it fell leaving the land of its power. Tajiki moved in from the north while the general Gul Agha Sherzai advanced from the south in Afghanistan. The Taliban forces moved to Pakistan while the anti-Taliban convened at the United Nations. With closed doors by the U.S., Karzai was elected to be the country's leader.

The man hunt for Osama bin Laden was undertaken. The Americans were the closest to bin Laden; in fact President Clinton was asked but denied the order. He slipped into Pakistan with the help of Afghan in conjunction with military forces. U.S. forces combined an attack on a cave complex. Al-Qaeda established a counter of operations in relation of the Pakistan northwest border with Afghanistan; Quetta was the town where the Taliban resided. One of the major battles in March 2002 which involved U.S. and Afghan forces, was the battle of the militants. This battle brought other countries which pounded special assets from several allied countries.

Despite tasking from several U.S. allies, the United States did not promulgate foreign forces to deploy in the Kabul area. The Pentagon ordered a soft imprint on Afghan soil or if the attention was placed on Iraq. International Security Assistance Force (ISAF) after seeking its efforts beyond Kabul, its ability to overcome failed when only a handful failed due to restrictions permitting full scale combat against Taliban and al-Qaeda. Even NATO foiled its mission by crippling of force due to a lack of scared armed soldiers. Base on international confidence in Afghanistan was dwindling.

The United States representative the largest foreign force in Afghanistan but it suffered greatly. One thousand troops were staged, particularly 300 deaths were recorded by the British. As the years ambled on more losses were suffered as the western nations' loss of faith became of leaving the troops under the gun.

Defense Secretary Donald Rumsfeld and our world leader, President George W. Bush stated that our major battles have ended in Iraq. In 2004 an overwhelming election gave Karzai a five year sweep as president. This election gave Afghanistan a strong government – weak and demoralizing people which was in contrary to this country's heritage.

TALIBAN RESURGENCE

Beginning in 2005 violence climbed to a new level by the Taliban using suicide bombs as buried bombs or Improvised explosive devices (IEDs). This tactic was never tried before but it managed and the death toll increased by November 2007. Many people (70 people) in Baghdad were killed and at the Indian embassy in Kabala. The Afghan government placed a warning that Pakistan was responsible for the heinous deaths.

By the Afghans' slowness of reconstruction and numerous prisoner abuses at U.S. detention prisons this promoted U.S. vehicles running into Afghans. NATO assumed control and the U.S. would play a smaller role in the conflict. This turn-about offered more boots on the ground especially in Iraq. This shift where bigoted person creating warfare was reaching disastrous problems, Washington thought the troops were ahead in the war.

Afghanistan was adept to the money grabbing opium! Western-backed challenged the use of opium and wanted to cultivate corps which would brighten their livelihood. This fell like wood in the forest – Afghanistan had 90% of the world's opium!

The United States has limited success in killing the Taliban. In early 2007 there have been killings of two Taliban leaders so the U.S. beginning to deploy drones (unmanned aerial planes). The U.S. after pleading to step the use of drones, the use of them was expanded in tribal areas in Pakistan to as far north as Balochistan.

THE OBAMA SURGE

When President Barack Obama was elected he sent additional troops to 36,000 U.S. troops and 32,000 NATO service members already there. He replaced General David McKiernan with General Stanley McChrystal in Afghanistan. General McChrystal's new strategy was ideal to the one raised in Iraq. They also persuaded enemy fighters to encourage reconsideration between Karzai and the Taliban leaders of government.

General McChrystal recommended that the new strategy he was embarking on needed more soldiers. He predicted that the war would suffer a great ruin if there was no surge in troop levels. After the second review of the pieces by President Obama, he ordered that a major reduction of forces was to happen in Afghanistan. Thus, a surge of drone strikes in Pakistan, President Obama visited Afghanistan to visit/speak to Karzai, and vowed in his inaugural address that he would stomp out inefficiencies of government – he did not achieve this in the short term remaining.

Karzai invited Mullah Omar the Taliban leader, but he declined. Karzai was scheduled to visit the White House but the meeting solidified the agreement to mend their relationship. The military command changed hands when President Obama fired McChrystal with General David Petraeus. McChrystal and his aides made remarks to the *Rolling Stone*; they discussed prominent leaders of the administration.

48

Comments about these offices were not complementary. President Obama explained that the charge would give General Petraeus to continue emphasis on protecting the Afghan people from rebellious tyrants and preventing civilian casualties.

Developments of the final objectives dealt with apprehending Al-Qaeda and dealing with Taliban. After locating him in Abbottabad in a secure compound, bin Laden was found and killed on May 2, 2011. A raid consisted of a helicopter which landed with Navy Seals which completed the job. The Secretary of Defense confirmed that the U.S. Government was meeting with the Taliban. On May 2, 2011, Bin Laden was killed. President Obama laid out a plan of reducing the military, saying it had attained a desired end by killing Al-Qaeda's leader and many of his cutthroats. This cut in strength left none in 2014 – a complete retreat! France thought likewise, removing troops as a former Afghan president was assassinated by an unknown suicide fanatic.

A series of inhumane incidents in 2012 provoked outrage within the United States and the Afghan government. U.S. Marines urinating on dead Afghans, disposing of the Quran and burning them. On March 11 a U.S. soldier went on a sporting spree – killing 17 Afghans. This happening caused forces widespread prolific acts related to words of Karzai. In a matter of days the Taliban broke out talks with the Allied countries. Later NATO effort will inactive when Afghan turned fire on them. These massacres caused new and more vigorous screening and also counseled turning to those men of certain soldiers.

The basic problem is the friction between President Obama and President Karzai. They settled on two agreements. The first was to transfer Afghan prisoners that were incarcerated by the U.S. to Afghan for safekeeping. The second, the Afghan forces were to land troops at night to capture or kill Taliban leaders. The raids brought benefit to U.S. troops but formed little success when violated private homes caused concern which destroyed this strategy increasing more rebellion.

The agreements in May 2014 cleared the way for outlining a clear path of night raids, etc., and the withdrawal of NATO troops. In 2014 it was problematic whether the U.S. would supply military support of if the Allied forces would supply men, run military trainers and act as informers. Foreign troops in a country after NATO combat cops remained unresolved until 2014. Karzai refused to sign the Bilateral Security Agreement before leaving office. Ashraf Ghani became the president when he immediately signed the agreement. This proclamation permitted 13,000 men to remain in country. U.S. and NATO formally ended combat action in Afghanistan on December 28, 2014.

MISTAKES OF THE AFGHANISTAN WAR

1. The Afghanistan conflict lasted way too long. The battle lasted 13 years going on forever!

2. In 2011, Afghanistan was handed to military police forces to counsel the attacks. It did not succeed because a number of incidents followed – they were ill-prepared!

3. From the Amu River the Russians came into Afghan territory. The U.S / Saudi did nothing but finally they led the Red Army to leave after ten years in country.

4. President Clinton knew where bin Laden was, but did not react. He denied the action!

5. With President Karzai being elected the turnabout of the enemy was expected. Due to weak government his support was weak and demoralizing!

6. The enactment of and the use of drones were concentrated in Pakistan. The use of drones was to be used in both Afghanistan and Pakistan.

7. General Stanley McChrystal was fired because of his strategy that worked. He asked for more soldiers when President Obama fired him.

8. When bin Laden was killed, President Obama declared he was responsible for his death. Seal Team six was responsible for his killing, Army pilots were dedicated to fly the helicopters, and so many on the ground who totally had a part in his death.

CHAPTER 8:

WAR IN IRAQ

THE WAR BEGINS

On March 2003 the United States along with allied or coalition assets began the war on Iraq. After thundering explosives rocked Baghdad, the capital of Iraq, U.S. President Bush announced that military forces are beginning to commence the disarming of Iraq, to free its people and to defend the world from harm. Saddam Hussein, the dictator, was in the process of building weapons of mass destruction (WMDs). This involved in an edict that Saddam and his sons Uday and Qusay, surrender and leave Iraq within 48 hours. On March 28th the first skirmish between the U.S. and Iraqi forces started. Seven terrific raids were recorded with high speed in Baghdad.

The first targets which were highly strategic areas were hit by the Tomahawk cruise missiles fired by the U.S. Navy warships positioned in the Persian Gulf. Air support was evident as fighters-bombers also hit zones of action. The Republic of Iraq in Baghdad spoke regarding the enemies of God had committed the act of aggression against our land and our people.

From the day of battle first marine expedition force, the third infantry Division plus the American forces set forth on Iraq. The eyes of Saddam Hussein's head that theme was they could take consulates. His idea of tactical empowerment was to use a similar South party Vietcong – to harass our troops which tend to undermine our troops. Para-military, or use of U.S. military informants, dressed in civilian clothes and when they let their guard down, they fling off their masquerade and appeared with AK-47 blazing.

So, in the first week of battle, it had cast a cloud over this prediction. Southern Iraqis have shown our troops that the Shiite majority is particularly excruciating gain, pain and overall harassment on our troops. This statement was not planned in route to Baghdad! Let's look at the troops – showing of the convoy's advance. The hurried forward of the American troops have left a spearhead over troops 30 miles from their base. Filled with precious fuel and ammunition they started to re-supply them, particularly the A-1 tanks and all fighting elements. For the most part they reached a point of no return as they were stymied because the Iraqi soldiers began their incessant ambushing of the force. Bands of soldiers capitalized on blitz-type encounters. The best thing the army called for was the Char gunships used to counter attack and return for more firepower or missiles.

Thus the second week of advancement toward Baghdad had stalled. Now it would take weeks before additional combat troops replenished the combat soldiers.

A supply clerk (a female) who was traveling in a humvee, was blown up about half the distance to Baghdad. The convoy got hit, she was thrown, lost and came under fire as the humvee crashed out of the convoy and was the only survivor of the incident. She was captured, beaten, questioned regardless of her injuries. A little more than seven months later she was rescued and turned over to the American military hospital. She became an icon of courage and purported "she was fighting to the death."

The delivery of Baghdad and a month of fighting left an army that is lacking of electricity, fresh water and dire need for medical care. By and large, the area surrounded in the sandy area is equal to the size of California. The speed of inva-sion caused them to use this as an everyday tactic!

Baghdad was surrounded by hospitals and you guessed it – mosques! The cen-ter of a town is dominated by many of Saddam Hussein's loyalists within many government buildings interspersed with military buildings. Our airplanes have bombarded these with Tomahawk missiles or laser-guided munitions which are launched by submarines or surface ships.

Three days later and still no relief, the search for the weapons takes to new techniques. All of the mechanisms sent to Iraq were potentially known as "troop killer." With more than 130,000 men spread all over Iraq the enemy is having a field day holding roadside attacks. These guerrilla attacks have made chili out of the use of armored or "heavy Humvees!"

The report made by the 101st Airborne Division recommends the use of the 50 caliber machine gun in the rear turret!

Virtually all escorts must be considered as possible targets. The first sign is when they see our Iraqi talking on a cell phone – an attack is close at hand! Guerillas attack the Humvee; shoot out the window of the thin-skinned side doors of the vehicle. In another case, the assault leads to rocket propelled grenades which come from the opposite side of the road. Another favorite tactic involves a device called the improvised explosive device (IED) made of artillery rounds, plastic used of hospitals' chemical transformation or a mixture of fertilizer and diesel fuel.

The aftermath and the end result of the failure of United Nations Monitoring Verification and the Inspection Commission (UNMOVIC) and the United States led Iraq to locate stockpiles of weapons of mass destruction (WMD) before and after the invasion of Iraq. The United States involvement was terminated in the search for unconventional arms in January 2005. This was concluded that this hypothesis of conventional weapons indeed did not exist!

Various agencies explored possible evidence that some or all of the WMDs were deceiving intelligence sources. Other conspiracy theories and second guessing all brought to explain the secret hiding locations.

According to MSNBC's *Hardball* in June 2005 the Iraqis "had a lot of time to move stuff." Numerous correspondence disavowed particular theories which amounted to a "hill of beans!" A former Pentagon investigator alleged he found this substance in 2003. But he reports they were laughed at were later destroyed by the CIA. This propelled was moved by Russia, Iraq and Syria who moved the WMDs to Syria. This was unlikely, and the massive list of stockpiles of arms was destroyed long before the war started.

Stockpiles were collected by Russia and prepared the removal of chemical weapons for Libya which was 30 years or three decades. Russians then turned to help Saddam whereby they destroyed, hid or transferred these weapons prior to the American invasion of 2003.

John Loftus of the Intelligence Summit said that many Iraq people testified that the WMDs were moved to Syria. By another source, the chemical and biological were transferred by airplane or by ambulance.

By late 2002 Saddam ordered all incendiary weapons including chemical stores moved to Syria. Thus they were transported by air or by ground elements. The WMDs were soon released as they were in tunnels under the town of Al-Baida near the city of Hawa. This placement was ordered by Saddam Hussein's Iraq Republican Guard! The Secretary of State Condoleezza Rice responded, "I don't think we are at the point that we can't make a judgment of this issue. There has not been any hard evidence that such a thing happened. But obviously we're going to follow up every lead, and it would be a serious problem if that, in fact, did happen!"

The Iraq survey Group removed guards and replaced them with intelligence people who supervised the banned materials between Iraq and Syria, which was reported in the *Washington Times*. The topic of interest, James E. Clapper, reported through intelligence and satellite imagery tracked numerous tracks, civilian carriers headed west from Iraq to Syria. All in all reasoning or specific radio analysis, the movement of WMD-related materials was proven without a doubt!

Al-Qaeda links planned and executed a chemical attack on Jordan. A truck entered Jordan from Syria with 20 tons of explosives. However, the truck contains possibly an explosive bomb or a large amount of sulfuric acid which can be used as a blister agent. This theory was explained why the Syrians gave their shipment to Al-Qaeda.

The *World Tribune* stated that in 2003 Iraq's WMD were moved to the Bekaa Valley which is a highly fortified stronghold. That leads to a bulk of chemical and biological weapons all being protected by Syria, Iraq helping them, and are in placed in the Bekaa Valley. Russia played a hand in the bowl or they used the "Spetsnaz, special forces," moved the weapons and eradicated their existence.

United States Deputy Undersecretary of Defense John A. Shaw was granted a designation or secret meaning "the Russian "Clean-up" operation was a "masterpiece of military camouflage and deception."

Former U.S. deputy Commander Lt. General Michael DeLong claimed that some of this material leaked into Iran. He and John Loftus gained knowledge that Iran had illicit weapons or the makings thereof.

The former head of Pakistan has admitted that his country assisted in shifting these arms to his country. This was verified as false data.

Saddam Hussein went into hiding, as the troops were driving the American invasion. He kept his people aware of his presence by releasing a specific audiotape. This command was withering away and capturing major cities in approximately three cities. Toppling the Saddam regime President Bush declared an end of major combat actions on May 1, 2003. Conventional military operations continued to battle insurgency ops. This broke the chain of Iraq. Another phase, guerilla warfare was number one on the minds of U.S. armed forces. This caused thousands of casualties and with civilians' deaths.

Saddam Hussein was captured on December 13, 2003, when he was asked about chemical and biological weapons, his replay was, "No, of course not, the U.S. dreamed them up itself to have a reason to go to war with us!" Later Saddam revealed that he had announced to his generals that there were no weapons of mass destruction. One theory, Saddam sent out different signals and different people to keep in power or retain the confusion level at its highest!

In early February many media reported U.S. forces had stormed a house in Baghdad. A computer disk contained a letter to a senior Al-Qaeda figure. An American Nick Berg was abducted and was beheaded by Iraq militants. This was thought as being Al-Qaeda work but was for the American abuse of Abu Ghraib prison.

Primarily ordered by the interim Iraq government, Operation Phantom P. Frig is a joint led U.S. Iraq attack against stubborn Fallujah. This attack claimed a victory for the U.S. but comes at a cost. The Red Cross claims that 800 Iraq civilians lost their lives. In December U.S. used white phosphorus to defeat the insurgents.

On December 8, 2004 Secretary Donald Rumsfeld commented about their impounded vehicles. This reacted to going into battle with unauthorized conflict with crippled armor. This was called "hillbilly armor."

In January 30, 2005, Iraq held its first democratic election. With sporadic riots with Sunni boycott, this turnout was high. Jalal Talabani was elected president, which the Bush administration considered the election as a major milestone.

In March the nine member commission approved by President Bush to analyze the U.S. Intelligence failures. The result of this panel concluded that not one bit of previous intelligence could be confirmed at the war's end.

Exactly a month after the Vice President Cheney gave his rosy review of the Iraqi tactics. Rumsfeld was upset when his views contradicted the Vice President's. His complaint is that the goal is to set up an environment to have successes in the long-term against the insurgence. On November 17, 2005, Representative John Murtha (D-PA) called for a resolution calling for the immediate redeployment of all United States forces from Iraq. This places all force balk at house will cause Iraq security matters in their own hands.

Representative Murtha's vocal blast to war strategy with help the Democrats regain control of matters and Congress during the elections.

In late October 2006 a new semantic battle occurred in Iraq. Between the Democrats and Republicans the administration evaluates and they agree about how to proceed as well as the White House continues its "Staying the course." When ABC News questions President Bush about this, he states he denies his strategy has ever been even staying on the course. Press Secretary Tony Snow soon gets boggled! Within a few months the tips turn strategy remains the same except when it proclaims a new technique – a surge strategy.

Around the same time, the government officials pursue that Iran is providing violence in Iraq. The U.S. Military shows evidence that Iran is shuttling information on technology on improvised explosives devices to Iraq. This causes concern with dispatches an aircraft carrier and an anti-missile battery in the Persian Gulf. In early March a regional conference involving security in Iraq which involves Iran.

On April 11, 2007, the Defense Secretary Robert Gates called for a three month extension of duty in Afghanistan. That same day the retired generals have refused to be the war czar. Republican Senator John McCain took a tour of Iraq including the full picture of what is going on here. Senator Barack Obama argues that Senator McCain had 100 soldiers, three Blackhawks and many other gunships with flak jackets contradict his analysis!

General David Petraeus on Capitol Hill reports on the progress about the new surge idea. This turnabout reveals there may be a reduction in troops. The Iraqi view is not in concert and refutes there has not been any valid progress. President Bush, on the sixth anniversary of 9/11, echoes Petraeus' testimony by endorsing a reduction in troop levels. This lowering of soldiers amounts to a current high of 169,000 to a cut of 130,000 armed men.

Political plots over the Iraq War are reaching Mount Everest. In order to evaluate this outbreak, General David Petraeus devises a much needed speech to Congress on April 8 and 9. He and Iraq ambassador Ryan Crocker agree that lowering the troops may reap disastrous happenings. His message was overshadowed by the three primary candidates running for president of the United States. Senator McCain calls the 140,000 men stay and we can look forward to success. Senator Obama calls the war a "massive strategic blunder!"

On September 1, 2008, the Iraq police took over the nation's Anbar providence. This was the Sunnis' warlord and now home to 25,000 troops. The Bush presidency claimed a milestone when they defeated a\Al-Qaeda extremist won by the Sunni Sheikhs. Anbar is the eleventh of eighteen returned, yet it is the Sunni provisions to be handed over. General Petraeus used the word victory, but two weeks later he was relieved by General Raymond Odierno in a government ceremony presided over by Defense Secretary Robert Gates. General Odierno echoes his relief in that these military gains were fragile, our walk is far from being complete.

On February 27, 2009, President Obama fulfilled his many campaign edicts by announcing to pull out his troops in Iraq by August 2010 and all of the American soldiers in the end of 2011. Some in his party are upset that the troops he leaves behind in 2001, 35,000 to 50,000 initially, President Obama gets some taking by collecting his election man John McCain who is cautious in promoting this plan. The President explains that his plan is so everyone although those you are complaining are "maybe were not paying attention." Being blunt his plan is stretched over 19 months instead of 16; he improvised during the election race. Not looking back about the war he is cautions because the troops may be coming home; however, the president has also vowed to actually boost troop levels in Afghanistan.

MISTAKES IN THE IRAQ WAR

1. The advanced attacks to Bagdad further than the supply could maintain them. A humvee, a female supply clerk was blown clear when the truck was detonated, was turned over and was captured by the Iraqis. They captured the young lady who was tortured and detained until unleashed to the U.S. Army. She was later believed a West Virginia hero!

2. The humvee was useless in this conflict. Their bodies particularly the underbody areas were demolished by the IEDs, the thin skin doors, and the rocket propelled grenades came from the opposite side of the driver's side.

3. Weapons of mass destruction were a topic of conversation. But the WMDs were moved to Syria. Technically President Bush did not know of their movement. Even Secretary of State Condoleezza Rice did not realize that this sudden movement had taken place. The displacement of WMD-related materials had, without a doubt, moved to Syria.

4. Iran has been undermining the help/aid of Iraq by shuttling technology on improved explosive devices. In March, a regional conference involving security which pointedly aimed at Iran.

5. A configuration existed among one general, President Obama and a running opponent, U.S. Senator McClain. The Senator called for 140,000 men which supports General Petraeus as the President called it "a massive strategic blunder!"

6. President Obama plans to withdraw the troops to the tune of 35,000 in 2011. This causes concern and it believes Iraq will thrive with an evil with more trouble in Iraq.

CHAPTER 9: ISLAM:

RELIGION OF PEACE OR WAR

The World Trade Center north tower in Manhattan was enjoying a fantastic morning from the 94th floor. A massive Boeing 767 with engines roaring was headed straight towards it. Minutes later they had been hit, which involved death, chaos and jet fuel had ravaged the World Trade Center buildings. The September 11, 2001 surprise attack killed almost 3,000 people by Islamist terrorist. The people on four airplanes, the people at work in the twin towers and the Pentagon in Washington, DC, were killed – their images are forever on our minds. Nothing can cure the regret of people leaping from skyscraper windows nor can we forget the massive cloud of debris as it choked New York City!

The world suffered when they heard of the tragic happenings in American. In many nations of Islamic faith celebrations were rampant. They brought out the American flags and burned them in effigy. Standing at the Islamic Center in Washington D.C., President Bush said that he proclaimed to a watching world that Islam was a peaceful growing religion. How can we, American people, believe that beheading and hatred by Islamic people, believe this is a religion of peace? We will attempt to answer this profound question.

The Terrorists of Islam state that the world is divided into two parts. Dar al-Harb is the house of war and Dar al-Islam is the house of Islam. A person is committed to the tearing or the sayings of their prophet. If he does not he is at war with Islam. Middle ground, that is no such follower?

Through all records we must understand who Muhammad was according to the holy of holy book of Islam. He followed the Quran, the Sunnah and the sayings or deeds of Muhammad. The predominant practice was the belief that waging holy war was called jihad.

Who was the god of Muhammad? Born in Mecca, in the Arabian Peninsula, A.D. 570, lies where the land of Saudi Arabia is today. Christianity and Judaism was around, even the Queen of Sheba came from this area. Belief in supernatural things like angels, demons, which lead to creatures called Jinn. During this period known as the Dark Ages, the Roman Empire fell. Even the seventh century known as the Renaissance, the Arabs seemed caught up in the millennium.

The boy Muhammad entered frequent trances brought about to demon possession. Raised by his uncle, the experiences he regained repeated tragedies.

A wealthy widow named Khadijah married Muhammad. He worked closely with his wife and encountered many Jews and Christians whereby he understood their beliefs and culture. Even at age 40 he still developed trances which asserted they grabbed him so tightly he obliged was in danger! Then this ghost-like creature experienced things which must be attributed to a Jinn! His wife and her cousin, Waraqa realized that he has been visited by a messenger of God as Moses who received a great law. According to Waraqa, he was considered a new prophet for his people.

The reign of terror by Muhammad's troops targeted all of Arabia, including Jews and Christians. All teenage children boys were killed as they dug a ditch and proceeded to behead 100 heads into the ditch. These awful readings of the Quran, because about us the "revelation" changed based on the circumstances of his tormented life. The idea was the "Doctrine of Abrogation," which means "annulment which replaces an old one."

We do not abrogate a verse or cause it to be forgotten except that we bring future one better than it or similar to it. So you not know that Allah is over all things complete?

Here are a few relationships he lorded from Allah:

- Muhammad put himself with Allah on terms of obedience whereby in the Quran the command that people obey without mentioning obeying Allah.

- He lusted after his adopted son or Zayd's wife.

- His unwanted sex and sexual slaves were also justified by Allah.

- Women were like any normal being as they were taken in possession in conflict.

- Muhammad ordered the best fifth of the spoils of battle (including women) were set aside for him.

- Muhammad thought the treasure of a defeated town was withholding information regarding the city's money.

In other words, Jesus Christ gave his life as a sacrifice for all. The Islam chief saved his life by sacrificing his own appetite and selfish gain.

JIHAD

Once Mecca was controlled, the Quran verses changed yet again. By and large they reverted to go or the offensive, kill infidels, and force Christians and Jews into Islam. This type is called "the verse of the sword." The Isaiah 47:4 of the Quran states the 21st century of the beheadings that has recently shocked the world.

MILITARY EXPANSION

Armed with weapons and a battle cry, they have raged an unparalleled reign of terror. The first target is the Arabian Peninsula. From this moment on we now called it Sharia Law. Starting in a 100 year period the forces of Islam roared the North Africa, Palestine, the Holy Land, and all parts of Europe and were stopped by Charles Martel in the Battle of Tours 732 A.D.

The killings reached on abominable statistics, beginning with known conquests:

51 million Christians
80 million Hindus
10 million Buddhist
25 million African people

Modern Muslims contend that Jihad relates to the innate struggle against human soul via temptation and the evil of a spiritual evil. When they announce "Jihad," this time they are building up their troops to encompass a wage of battle for the soul.

According to Islam those who participate in Jihad will be assured that if one dies his death will be by Allah and his being will be mercy throughout what he will have on earth.

Allah controls Muslins to carry out jihad. In fact, those who don't perform will go to hell. Muslims are true individuals that abide jihad. In fact, Allah performs forgiveness and commands his followers by beheading people. There are many rules; some require the cutting of necks and fingers if they oppose the teachings of Allah and Muhammad.

These are a few of the heinous teachings of the Quran. Today the world is plagued by the Muslim Brotherhood harassing, and murdering non-Muslims across the world. The Western mind cannot dream of such bigotry of the Muslim-led society. This is not the Christian and Jewish way of predicated on murderous bombs sending its children into minefields causing a null and void as a comment to their god!

So, is Islam a religion of peace or war? Profoundly from the teaching of leading imams all around the world today, the evolution of Islam offers the submission of all people to itself! When submission confronts freedom, there is only one inevitable outcome. The obvious answer is war!

CHAPTER 10:

TERRORISM ON THE RISE

The terrorist attack of 9/11 marked a destructive surprise which began in the 1980s. The truck bombing, a French military barracks produced 295 lives which reveal the deadly feat of terrorism. Be it a fact, the number produced ten times higher than those of the 1983 barracks conflict.

The Federal Bureau of Investigation (FBI) equates or divides the violence in the United States as domestic and international. Domestic terrorism is the unlawful or threatened by the group or personalities based within the USA. This is without foreign distinction towards persons or property to coerce a government, the civilian population, or any way this further finances of political or social objectives.

International terrorism defines violates or acts dangerous to human lives or violation of criminal laws of the USA or any states. Also, the criminal violation of communities within the jurisdiction of the USA or any state is warned. These acts are intended and will coerce the population; affect the policy of the government, and affect the overall conduct of this government. Acts which transient boundaries in which they accomplished previous appear to intimidate or the local neighborhood where perpetrators exist. By and large, domestic and international terror organizations represent threats to American within the borders of the United States.

Improved analysis to operational tasks have brought affluence of data that leave enhanced the FBI's ability to investigate, predict violent occurrences and prevent actual happening of terrorism. Despite the focus on all international disturbances will have to remain cognizant on all fronts within the United States of

America. Seeing September 11, 2001, the crashing of planes into the World trade Center, the invasion of the Pentagon, and the crash in a field in Pennsylvania, this caused more casualties than have ever recorded.

FBI guards the country in preventing acts of violence in American. The FBI has installed a broad-based counterterrorism program based on previous intent to disrupt effective warning. This will help developing the warning which will quell the most effective response.

Now, let's consider our most prevalent terror groups!

BOKO HARAM – NIGERIA'S ISLAM INSURGENCY

An Islam extreme group which has murdered dozens of civilians and girls has been Boko Haram. A suicide bomber dressed as a high school student detonated explosives killing fifty students and teachers. Quickly suspicion reverted on Boko Haram, which had created a pattern of annihilation in this part of the country.

The militants sought to its horrendous attacks since Nigeria announced a stand-off since 250 school girls were taken away. As a result the spokesmen of the suicide group said that no use fires and the girls kidnapped would not return. In fact, the speaker was quoted, as they have now accepted Islam, married, and the release of these girls is preposterous.

The bloody bombing and kidnapping are unstoppable! They often engage the Nigerian forces. This promotes establishing an Islamic caliphate after ultimately overthrowing the government.

The October the agreement of a conceived plot, 60 young women were kidnapped in another in control of Boko Haram. Yes, there were numerous attacks that followed. Now in its sixth year of its agreement, he has not stopped this insurgency. He started this killing and hostage taking in 2002 in Maiduguri by the Muslim cleric Mohammed Yosef. The northern part was controlled by Boko Haram united with the help of Al-Qaeda which he controlled the terrorist organization in western Africa. Clashes between Muslims and Christians were common in Nigeria where the group's founder was killed by Nigerian police in 2004. Thus, this group went underground with unbelieving, out of the night violence!

Since then their leader carried out lethal attacks on every hostile building including villages, government houses and police buildings and including mosques. In 2011 these attacks spread to many parts of the country, including the capital Abuja. This incident almost killed several dozen people while a car detonated near the United Nations headquarters.

In 2012 he touched attacks in Kumo which made it the deadliest blow. Another, deadly strike was in Maiduguri where 500 died and it was recorded that Boko kicked as if it were a jailbreak attempt by them. Other incidents were:

a.   The militants attacked schools which were commended as "Western education is forbidden."

b.   Last February he slaughtered 50 teenager students.

c.   April 15 in Chibok; the soldiers marched into a girl's school and left with 250, loaded them into a truck and left them in a dense forest at night. The President Jonathan began to take action, but the women wanted to take back our girls.

The situation worsened as a Human Rights Watch report unleashed a report containing the 500 women and the like subject to Boko Haram began its torture since 2009. What will Boko Haram then do?

The lies and other actions by President Barak Obama, Secretary of State Hillary Clinton, and Susan Rice (the president's National Security Advisor), were full of prevarication and very monstrous. The divining the truth, the risk of Benghazi's real happenings, Obama's administration pretended the attack had nothing to indicate terrorism.

CHAPTER 11: PALESTINE

There was never or any fallacies did of our parent or past time did Israel steal the land called Palestine. The land will never be their land! The Jewish people received this land as stated in the Bible yet will remain the Jewish people in perpetuity. Despite 27 invasions of Judea and Samaria withstanding conquests, exiles, massive oppression, and acquiescence by Jews themselves, they survived and what is known in Hebrew as Israel. These people have turned a desert into a little democracy, the envy of the world.

The facts show otherwise. Israel is one of many open societies in the universe! 6.7 million is the population, 1.1 million are Muslims. 130,000 are Christians and 100,000 are Druze. All have equal voting rights including Arab women! Myth: The Palestine Authority protects Jewish Holy sites.

Just in years 1996 – 2000:

- September 1996, Palestine rioters destroyed a synagogue at Joseph's Tomb in Nablus.

- Rachel's Tomb near Bethlehem was attacked in 1996.

- October 2000, Joseph's Tomb was burned particularly after the Israel guard was withdrawn. This tomb was rebuilt as a mosque.

- October 2000, the ancient synagogue in Jericho was destroyed; however, it was rebuilt but it was damaged.

When was Palestine recognized by any country? The defaming of Israel lacks real basis for historical facts. Where would it be founded (Palestine)? Where is its borders, and what is the name of its capitol? What is the basis of the economy and what form of government existed? What finally was its religion?

At no recorded time in history has there ever been a nation called Palestine. During 1299 – 1922 the Ottoman Empire where this land was dubbed by the Romans, then the Turks – there was never an outcry for a Palestine State. The illegal domination of Judea and Samaria was overtaken by the Hashemite kingdom of Jordan before 1949. An armistice developed and prior to 1967, the mention neither of "occupied territory" nor of a Palestine State. Why did Israel's unattainable conquest in the six day war, a mark unprovoked by Israel? The mystery continues as a nation victorious in battle and is expected to be vanished and the world to see for peace. Not only peace, but to cede land and that was their own. Should Israel kneel to Palestine demands that the land won in conflict?

With the exception of the United States, it was the countries like Diaspora, were forced to flee from repression and join the clan who maintained a 3,000 year existence in Judea, Samaria and the adjoining areas. Does this smell without disagreement? The Jewish people were thrown out of Jerusalem, Judea and Samaria by the Babylonians. They returned to their homeland, rebuilt the second temple, burned again and again exiled from their abode.

After numerous conflicts and conquests, before King David and Solomon, the Jews have invariably connections to the land. Having controlled this terra firma, where all the Jews from Poland, The Ukraine? Russia? Anyone who can believe or understand this fluff should stop this before our children with venom believe this.

We can go on with history, boys and persecution! Certainly the Jewish people have a legitimate claim to their ancient homeland. They certainly, hands down, have more than the so-called Palestine. Arabs do. After a thousand of years, the world at large can't bear to see the Jewish people once again in charge of their own land and their own destiny?

CHAPTER 12:

HAMAS

BACKGROUND

In 1987 Ḥarakat al-Muqāwamah al-'Islāmiyyah Islamic Resistance Movement (HAMAS) was formed at the beginning of the initial Palestine intifada or beginning of its uprising. The roots are in the branch of Palestine's pledged to the Muslim faith. It is built up of a robust sociopolitical set up inside Palestine's boundaries. This group called for an establishment which constitutes an Islamic Palestine state which pushes out Israel and trashes all agreements, documents made between the Palestine Liberation Organization (PLO) and Israel. HAMAS is concentrated in the Gaza Strip or in the areas of the West Bank.

The military branch of HAMAS is known as the Izz ad-Din al-Qassam Brigades that is prominent in anti-Israel attacks either or in Israel or Palestine territories since 1990. These attacks range from large scale movements including bombings against civilian targets, small shootings incidents, IED (Improvised explosive devices) and other heinous attacks. In early 2006 various elections in the Palestine sectors ending the secular Fatah priority which challenging this part's overwhelming leadership of this Palestine national movement. All through 2008 HAMAS explores the refusal to abide or renounce violent action against Israel which included suicide bombings and unknown rocket and similar mortar attacks which have maimed people injured. This caused the United States government to designate the HAMAS organization as a Foreign Terrorist Organization.

HAMAS after many meetings entered into an alliance with Israel in 2008 which gained a six month agreement which curtailed many rocket incidents. Following this temporary calm the masked attacks accelerated which precipitated a major Israel military operation in late December.

2008

After destroying the HAMAS military might in the Gaza Strip, Israel declared a cease-fire on January 18, 2008.

HAMAS agreed in April 2011 plus Fatah reaffirming an interim government. HAMAS left its longtime political headquarters in Damascus and spread throughout the region as Syrian President Bashar al-Assad placed a crackdown in the country, made remaining in Syrian unlikely for the group. May 2012 HAMAS claimed a 300 force which was to prevent other Palestine resistance groups which fired missile-like weapons into Israel. Conflict broke out, which HAMAS worked to maintain this ceasefire by Egypt that ended. Other Palestine militants flouted ceasefire with sporadic conflicts throughout 2013 and 2014. Fatah and HAMAS decided to form a technocratic unity governed by Palestine Prime Minister Rami Hamdallah to hold conferences every six months.

HAMAS has not removed resistance against this terrible enemy Israel, while pursuing reconciliation with Fatah.

In July 2014 the unhappy claim between HAMAS and Israel was completely broken down when three Israeli boys were kidnapped and killed in the West Bank. The sleuths attributed to Israel to HAMAS – and a Palestinian was wasted by Israel settlers in the region. Retaliatory rockets by HAMAS' military wing and other Palestinians in the Gaza Strip escalated into the longest, most lethal and troublesome conflict with Israel since 2009.

HEZBOLLAH

Hezbollah– or the Party of God – is a most powerful political and military body in Lebanon consisting of Shia Muslims. Hezbollah is a Shia Islamist militant-political group based in Lebanon. Its primary paramilitary ring is called The Jihad Council and its loyalty is to the Loyalty in the Resistance Bloc located in Lebanese body. After the death of Abbas al-Musawi in 1992, his group was headed by Hassan Nasrallah.

It emerged with financial guidance from Iran in 1980. Its goal was to obliterate Israel troops for Lebanon. The party's main objective was to stoke the flames of

Hezbollah peaked during 2000 yet cut a huge dent in among Lebanese people. But it was the center of a homogenous war with Israel followed by the capture, torture of two soldiers of Israel in 2006.

Lebanon's pro-Syrian opposition was Hezbollah's big advantage as it was pitted against pro-western government, Saad Hariri. By many numerous seats in parliament he formed a national entity in 2009. This blocked the forming of a new president. The statement on May 21, 2008, reached a transaction and unified the power of veto was solidified!

Washington has recognized Hezbollah as a terrorist group and warned Lebanon that destruction in wake of Syria's action. This nation has hindered or withdrawal of forces with the assignation of former Lebanese Prime Minister Rafic Hariri!

Syrian blessing was long operated with neighboring guidance. The protection it has given support its involving Lebanon serving a trump card for Damascus. This, of course, plays its ace with Israel over the operation of the Golan Heights. "Western Interference" highlights Hezbollah's leaders have in support of Syria stressing Lebanese unity. Plus, it has popular appeal, coastline, social services and needs medical services.

Hezbollah's test came unexpected in 2006 by killing of his army leaving for dead two Israel with others left dead. This rough triggered a long standing war with Israel which ended in a ceasefire.

After surviving a massive onslaught, Hezbollah announces victory enhancing credibility in the Arab world. The critics sought a different verdict reached Israel weakened in Lebanon. Despite the United Nations resolutions (1559 passed in 2004 and 2007) caused the war), called for the disarming of militia in Lebanon and Hezbollah – this army remains intact!

The Hezbollah was generated in 1982 a contingence of 2,000 forces, Iranian Revolutionary guards were ordered to Lebanon's Bekaa Valley where they were directed to message Israel by aiding resistance. In essence, the army was to maintain or offering resistances to Jewish occupation, with dreams of transforming this state into an Iranian-style Islamic state. This did not materialize!

The party's rhetoric calls this annihilation of Israel. Apparently this fact could not hold forthwith. A Jewish empire has no right or any way to be equated to a Muslim entity. This party was well supported by Iran which be provided money and arms!

Hezbollah adapted to taking western hostages through freelance taking cells. In 1983 members went on to 1983 to provide suicide bombing training, which they attacked 241 United States marines in Beirut!

Hezbollah enjoyed the Islamic way of life. They imposed strict sanctions on rules of Islamic code on villages or towns in the country. But the party emphasis is the vision of Islam should be known. But its intention will not impose an Islamic society on the Lebanese!

CHAPTER 13:

AL-QAEDA IN THE ARABIAN PENINSULA (AQAP)

It is a militant or Islamic group "Givers of the Helpers of the Arabia," it is active in Yemen and Saudi Arabia. Named for Al-Qaeda but it is subordinate to the now deceased Osama bin Laden, who is from Saudi Arabia yet he is a citizen of Yemen. Due to other factors that ranking leadership, the AQAP is the deadliest branch which consecrates on attacking the enemy which increases the plotting on overseas targets! This group established as an Emirate during the 2011 revolution of Yemen.

A 2009 AQAP was solidified in January with the merger of Yemen and Saudi. The Saudi government was effectively halted causing all to suspend to Yemen. By 2010 it is believed to have at least several hundred members.

U.S. Secretary of State decreed and designed al-Qaeda as a terrorist in Yemen in December 14, 2009. The *Washington Post* stated that they organized in Yemen had suppressed its alive, Osama bin Laden elite group its most dangerous threat to the U.S.A. By August 2010, Yemen criticized the size and danger of al-Qaeda in Yemen. A former bodyguard for bin Laden warned of intense fighting between the two countries and predicted they would increase the interventions to remain in power. However, Ahmed Al Baki warned that apparently incidents that was characteristic of unit strength. Operations carried out in the Arabian Peninsula in 2009 – a drive-by shooting in Little Rock, AK, Abdulhakim Mujahid Muhammad, carried out a SRS Rife shooting on soldiers in front of a U.S. military recruiting situation, obviously a jihad bombardment.

He killed an army soldier who bore the burden for the terrorist attacks. The next incident was in Christmas time in Detroit, Michigan, 2009. Umar Farouk Abdulmutallab tried but his underwear had explosives which failed to ignite!

2010

On February 8, 2010, a deputy leader called for obstructing the Red Sea, which prevented ships from going to Israel. The cargo bombs were implanted onboard in October 29, 2010, on cargo planes. The packages were described to have originated from Yemen, to an address of two Jewish agencies in Chicago, Illinois. This verified that Al-Qaeda was the immediate candidate for this fault finding in the bombing of U.P.S. Boeing 747-400 which was from Dubai on September 3, 2010. Meanwhile the American authorities surmised that the perpetrator was Al-Qaeda, were designed to destroy subject airplanes. In late 2010, they announced that they concentrated on small-scale explosives intended to weaken the U.S. economy.

On May 21, 2012, a soldier bearing a belt of explosives carried out a suicide attack in response to a Yemen's Unity Day. AQAP claimed the incident in which 120 were dead and over 1,200 were maimed! And, if that wasn't enough, in June 2012 they planted land mines which killed 13 civilians after 3,000 mines were obscured in and around Zinjibar and Jaar.

2013

December 5, 2013, an attack on the Yemen's Defense Ministry involving 60 people. This crisis further extends the killings and maintaining Al-Qaeda's supreme announcement of random and harm to the Yemeni people.

2014

In 2014 the online political magazine well pushed the Voice of Jihad and Inspire. In December 2015 the Seals and Yemen Special Forces attempted to rescue when eight hostages were held in the balance. On December 6 the main forces using other nations kept trace of American Luke Somers and South African Pierre Korkie. When the U.S.A. finally entered the building, they found the two suspects hanging on to life. Somers and Pierre Korkie died shortly after the brave souls and other forces lost their lives.

2015

On January 7, 2015, the Al Qaeda assaulted the French newspaper *Charlie Hebdo*, resulting in more than eleven individuals put to death. Two days after the incident Al-Qaeda confirmed the attack on *Charlie Hebdo*. The reason was given to gain "revenge for the honor" of the Islamic Prophet Muhammad!

CHAPTER 14:

ISIS

In the light of global attacks of the past few months, most particularly the American people are not familiar with the group—ISIS. This term is synonymous with terror, violence and bloodshed. This causes continuously to increase in the Middle East, Africa, Liberia, England, and perhaps in the United States.

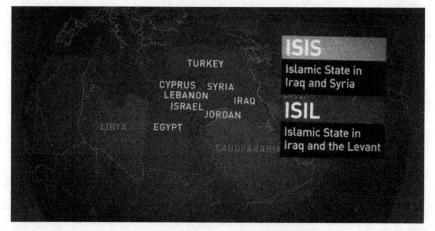

ISIS stands for Islamic State of Iraq and Syria or ISIL is Islamic State of Iraq and Levant. On June 14 it became known it renamed itself – Islamic State proclaims a creation of a global caliphate! The new caliph Abu Bakr al-Baghdadi was now ruling all Muslims. From this time on the new caliphate is head of all ISIS, ISK and IS which are synonymous.

ISIS was founded in 1999 by Abu Musab al-Zarqawi. Within five years he chose to follow the principles of Osama bin Laden and Al-Qaeda. The organization agreed that the group should be called Islamic extremist, Islamist or Jihadist. This was closely linked to Jihad or "struggle." Various groups such as the Taliban, Boko Haram, Al-Qaeda, Hamas and Hezbollah, separate groups are making news for decades, but ISIS is in a league of its own.

In 2010 Al-Qaeda left and dissociated itself from the ISIS. Al-Qaeda did not hold the honor of ISIS because it was too extreme. ISIS continues to grow and they have lived up to barbaric names. They continue the advance to the Middle East spreading to new heights.

THEIR IDEOLOGY

ISIS follows an extreme form of Islam know as Salafism, "pious forefathers." It maintains quranic hegemony through a severe adherence to the Quran and Sharia law. ISIS adheres to an apocalyptical theology and believes that the Muhammad will soon redeem Islam. ISIS declares jihad against all infidels. That includes westerners both Christian and Jews. But it includes Muslims who do not believe or pledge allegiance to the new caliphate – for example Hamas.

THEIR METHODS

After 18 months, ISIS has maintained their barbaric attitude and decorum. Described as a terrorist organization, they are known as a militia. This group is unusual where this sort of training where corruption, chaos, military and made Supreme Being are the highest. Recent beheading, rapes, and live burnings are done and paralyze the world into believing that they can't respond quickly. Additionally they use social networks or other means to spread their propaganda as well as gain new members all over the world.

ISIS represents a kind of Islam which permits savage violence. It continues to draw new members which go to the Middle East to train. Upon completion of the training scenario, they return to their respective nations; this moral spirit of life takes the dedicated ISIS to worship death and gives the world an act of human life is a challenge.

ISIS AND THE END TIMES

"One of the most shocking aspects of the rise of ISIS, particularly with regard to the horrifying murders it has committed, is the pure unadulterated hatred that has accompanied these gruesome acts." It says, if only ISIS members were not so poor; if only they had more jobs. If we look deeper we soon see and discover the views that they have of Christians and Judaism that must be silenced. Only one view can be realized, emerged victorious – according to ISIS, the final chapter is victory for Muhammad.

THE MAZE OF ISLAMIC ESCHATOLOGY

The Islamic eschatology is difficult to comprehend and surely will confuse those which have little or no knowledge in general or what Islam is in particular. The recent execution of 21 Coptic Christians shed some light on ISIS blood and motivation. Christianity is viewed as a threat to the ISIS dream of establishment of the future caliphate or the Islamic government.

Jesus is the central role is to put at all end of the Islamic theology. In their way of thinking, Jesus will put to end all religious other than Islam.

Finally, we must acknowledge that ISIS is not well understood according to the West. We must reconcile with the motivation that condones gruesome maiming of humans which all in religious belief that maybe the most convinced Christian or Jew. It is a fact that ISIS is a dangerous as if they are driven by their theology. First and foremost, we can through our reading, we thoroughly understand this threat.

Today we must pray for peace in Jerusalem or ISIS has its authority it will destroy or take our Israel. Neither Isaiah nor Jeremiah not of ISIS, but they do immediately say that the enemies would surround Israel.

"We worship a Savior who loved us all so much that he died for our sins and rose from the grave, conquering death. We serve an all-powerful God and we should not fear the future. We should look ahead knowing that what was foretold will come to pass. Our responsibility is to be His vessels of mercy and grace to all – to the Jew first and also to the Gentiles – including ISIS."

In reality the ISIS was born from Al-Qaeda, the Islamic State and Syria (ISIS) and has become the dominant power in recent years. Syria and Iraq demonized large regions which have become U.S. military operation which has cold blooded killers both in executions and dominates the killing of Westerners.

ISIS can trace its beginning with the Sunni Awakening, the collection of Iraq Seven tribes supported by the U.S. In 2011 the Syrian conflict started and later moved to Iraq in 2013. Al-Baghdadi changed the name to ISIS. President Obama referred to them as a "JV" team.

The success of ISIS of these terrorists as it cut its way from Syria, Iraq and into Baghdad showing military expertise. ISIS fighters turning and using all types

81

of executing many persons former service U.S. types that helped train Iraqi security forces, put up a good fight – taking advantage of government forces.

The Iraq force and much of its military are made up of Sharia Muslims and are retained where ISIS has predominately Sunni or ISIS. In other words, the Iraq forces are not operating in the same areas. ISIS has built relations with the Sunni and ex-Baathists because of the government in Baghdad. ISIS was handed its first defeat in 2014 when Iraq and Kurdish troops plus U.S. aerial bombing runs pushed the terror group off Mosul Dam.

The U.S.-led coalition expanded aggressive bombing runs against ISIS in September 2014. In February 2015 the military said that the ISIS is losing ground in Iraq.

Westerns have rough estimates on ISIS strength, but in 2014 she made 30,000 fighters strong. Most troubling is a huge portion leaves their houses and travel half way around the globe to join ISIS. The National Counterterrorism Center in February 2015 said some 20,000 foreign men from 90 countries went to join Syrians to join the group. To the U.S.A., 150 have either traveled to the conflict zone or attempted to do so.

Is ISIS a threat to our nation? Through bombing focused on targets, the head of ISIS has called on his followers to conduct deadly at home. In addition to "self-radicalized" supports the Western intelligence are concerned about those who travel to Syria and Iraq to fight before coming back home. The battlefields in Iraq and Syria provide foreign fighters with combat experience weapons and explosive, training and access to terrorist networks that may be planning attacks which target the West. Rasmussen said in February 2015. Incidentally they target and brutally murdered countless Christians either male or female.

GlobalPost American journalist was on assignment to cover the conflict in Syria. He was abducted and killed apparently on camera by a terror group – another American journalist Steven Sotloff was caught and was in President Obama hands. The U.S. continued to kill ISIS with dozens of airstrikes. The militant in black stood as he was executed. The execution was the first of many who died at the sword!

CHAPTER 15:

JUDICIAL WATCH ON ISIS THREAT ON BORDER

The issue of ISIS is right here in the United States of our government. The unheard of and inexplicable knowledge is the ISIS operations both here (USA) and Mexico. An ISIS camp is near El Paso, Texas; that includes a Mexican officer and a Mexican Federal police inspector.

The exact position of this terrorist camp is known as "Anapa" which is about eight miles from the U.S. border. This area is located just west of Ciudad Juarez in Mexico. Yet there is another cell in Puerto Palmas which promotes easy access to New Mexico towns, which unknown sources confirm.

During further joint tactical work, the authorities of the Mexican Army and federal officials discovered documents in Arabic and Hindu as plans of Fort Bliss, the military organization which houses U.S. Army 1st Armored Division. These documents were found in Muslim prayer rugs during this operation.

Law enforcement and spy's (often called intelligence) report that the town around Anapra is dominated by the Juarez Cartel, Sinaloa (the police arm of the cartel), and the Barrio Azteca which is a gang that was formed in the jails of El Paso. In essence, Mexican Army and Federal Police find it an enormously hazardous area to conduct terrorist operations with cartel control of the area.

According to the "coyotes" which are engaged in human smuggling, and working for the cartel, help transport the ISIS through the desert and across the border from Santa Teresa and Sunland Park, Acacia, New Mexico. To the east through the porous border near Fort Hancock, Texas the coyotes are capitalizing, smuggling ISIS terrorist. Numerous times these areas are highlighted because of understaffed municipal and county police forces. The safe-haven areas provide the unchecked super-areas where drug containment areas that are ongoing!

What is ISIS doing? They intend to exploit railways and airports in the vicinity of Santa Teresa, New Mexico, which is a USA port of entry. "Spotters" reveal that in Eastern Potrillo Mountains of New Mexico are assisting in border crossing. ISIS is conducting surveillance of the following sites: the White Sands Missile range; Alamogordo, NM government facilities; Ft. Bliss and the electrical power conduits near Anapra and Chaparral, NM.

Any action, global, territory or homeland security often surprises the Mexican government which has "categorically denied" all conclusion of the findings. This overcomes the blatant cover-up of Benghazi crowd supposed by the Obama center any day!

Without mathematical devices we are all hearing about the ISIS supporters that were arrested in a terror plot that was here in the USA. Twenty-five ISIS supporters were being prosecuted by the Supreme Justice Department. Bomb building was the two female carriers in New York and other were existences of both in Ohio and in Kansas. So, question, is ISIS presently all over America, with they have the advantages over the Mexican drug cartel?

With the FBI in action, the following is being investigated:

1. ISIS will be investigated by the FBI through a "Special" meeting between U.S. Consulate in Ciudad Juarez.

2. A high level source which must remain a secret, will meet to advocate who is the unknown culprit. Undoubtedly the contact will reveal the names of the victims. The FBI officers assigned to Mexico were "no absento," which finds it's absent unclear why the Homeland Security did not attend!

3. U.S. and Mexico have concluded that in the southern border, the DHS and rapid FBI brass seems to deny the report seems to indicate the findings indicate otherwise!

Derry Murdock related that the ISIS group trounced Iraq and Syria in pickup trucks, calling them the "JV." Senator Obama's lack of decision and daintiness let them size power and land – much more than envisioned. He knows or does he know of the teaming coup eight miles below the border in Mexico.

CHAPTER 16:

THE CONFUSED GUIDE TO THE SYRIAN CIVIL WAR

The French President called it "an act of war" against his country in which on November 13 staged a complex attack in Paris that left 129 dead. ISIS claimed the bombastic art citing the involvement in the "crusader companion," Syrian President Bashar al-Assad claiming we don't happen to take this incident lightly. France is one of 65 members in the U.S.-led international coalition against the Islamic state. They might point out that only eight members have conducted airstrikes against Syria.

France's involvement in Syria is recent, having numerous air attacks in Iraq and joined a list of Syria training camps by bombing the ISIS. France announced two days after the France debate, that it was bombing Raqqa, Syria; obviously the U.S. shares intelligence with French counterparts.

That Syrian disaster began with peaceful protests against, the government in 2011. It is a civil war against the people against the war with and which has increased featuring Russia and Iran against the U.S. and/or allies.

Whatever it has been, the killing ration is 220,000 and caused the rise of ISIS! So, the de facto international coalition makes informed allies of other be devoted to defeat ISIS on overlapping steps. Yet the Syrian war looked different as protagonists look at it!

WHO?

Most people want to know by one count from 2013, 13 or possibly more rebel units were operating in Syria. U.S. Defense Intelligence Agency puts groups at

1,200, where numerous groups like the United States have nine countries which have participated in U.S.-led air strikes against ISIS in Syria. For example, Canada's new Prime Minister has vowed to end his country's involvement, Russia conducting bombing against ISIS, and in coordination with Iran and Hezbollah fighters on the ground. Many countries have citizens who have joined ISIS and other soldiers in Syria.

Thomas van Linge had gained ground by detailed maps of the Syrian battle. His categories of groups are:

a.   Rebels (Moderate to Islamist)
b.   Loyalist (regime forces and their supporters)
c.   Kurdish groups (are not seeking to overthrow Assad)
d.   Foreign Powers

Many of the clans are fighting or claiming to overpower ISIS! The separation of the two is to keep Assad in Power (Iran and Russia) and they are focusing on the Islamic State (U.S. led coalition)!

Thus Russia has intervened on the loyalist side while the U.S.A has helped the rebels, yet the support identifies certain rebels providing arms and traveling to "vetted" groups. The contradiction is that America wants Assad to go, but since he is fighting ISIS, the strongest force in Syria, it is "the enemy of my enemy is my friend."

Principle: There, why is it difficult to wrap my head around our involvement in the conflict?

Russia's is less sensitive to the rebel groups – it opposes them all! Foreign Minister Sergey Lavrov said: "If it looks like a terrorist, acts like a terrorist and fights like a terrorist; it's a terrorist, right?"

THE BATTLE FOR SYRIA
Where?
What started in Syria spread to multiple countries – to Iraq where ISIS spread to and taken a chunk to the northwest. Turkey and Lebanon which together have more than three million registered Syria refugees. In Europe 500,000 asylum born in 2011 for Syria; and the United States have their share of 3,000 since 2011, yet 10,000 more of refugees are programmed for the next year.

Why?

Why did the protest of 2011 as a response to the arrest and mistreatment of young people accused of graffiti in southern city of Persia transform into today's abyss? The fight transpired when two Arabs in Tunisia and Egypt blamed pro-demonstrations. Syrians were not unique. The Syrian uprising performing as an opening of the opposition to Assad maybe be a short-term for political gains by taking up as before the Arab Spring vanished. Many events happened by releasing political prisoners and obstructing officials, but caused a disturbance which with pin-point reaction which would cause a national crisis which would deepen short of existing changes!

Once the war starts, keep it going! The *Atlantic*'s Dominic Tierney said and argued that Assad solely obtained to diminish the rebellion, by releasing terrorist formations which caused avoiding the fight with ISIS.

When?

Many question the many reader's questions: When does this war end? Barbara F. Walters enjoyed the civil wars have lasted ten years. Martin Libicki of the Rand Corporation purports that insurgencies end when outside state support is withdrawn with foreign involvement increasing on either side, neither is likely to win, or lose, in the predictable future.

SYRIA IN 60 SECONDS

Andrew Tabler, an expert at the Washington Institute for Near East Policy gives his view of the conflict:

> The Syria Civil War, the worse crisis since the World War II with over a quarter million killed, and half of Syria's 22 million people removed from their homes. Syria is the largest war field and is the generator of Sunni-Shia sectarianism the world has ever seen. These are deep implications for future boundaries of the Middle East and the spread of terrorism. What started was the regime of President Bashar al-Assad to claim the largest uprising that has existed. Three general areas which the U.S. designed this country; in the West we have the Alawite and Assad clan, Sharia militias trained and funded by Iran; in the center Sunni moderate, Islamist groups such as ISIS and al-Qaeda

share control. And, finally in the northeast the Kurdish-based People's Protection Units (YPG) have two of three territory divisions of a country.

Western Kurdistan as a country that have lost people where neighboring states have carved out based on sectarian agencies tear up the fabric of Syria. Iran (now Russia), Turkey, Jordan, Saudi Arabia, Qatar and the UAF are supporting the Sunni's opposition, and the Kurdistan (PKK) supporting the YPG enemy.

Chapter 17: Post Benghazi

It has been an insightful, closed doors and who knows what, where and why the specific debacle occurred. There are many testimonies that blame numerous people; including the President, Secretary of State and the list grows along the top echelons of our FBI, Central Intelligence Agency (CIA) and many more to humiliate.

President Obama act of administrative execute powers quickly eliminated General David Petraeus as Director of the CIA during what Hillary Clinton did as she transmitted e-mails unclassified which is in violation of the National Security Association. As you know by now, that General Petraeus became infuriated by how much he has gained when Hillary turned down for help, U.S. Ambassador Chris Steven's. She refused to added security for the U.S. Mission in Benghazi, over a five month period! (Redacted: To select or adapt by redlining or removing substantive information.)

Ambassador Stevens was sent up to die because of his gun-running child trade and drugs because the CIA to promote change in Libya using terrorist funded illicit leading out and was prior to the election. Apparently the Ambassador had to be muted! General Petraeus had to be put in a place where he was not forced to testify before Congress but he could not take the fifth!

Secretary Clinton was communicating to Ambassador Stevens where to provide extra protection which he desperately needed. Ambassador Stevens. Therefore. was working for the CIA which was headed by David Petraeus. General Petraeus would have obviously known of Ambassador Stevens' activities. To protect the president (for the 2012 election), both men had to go!

People were wondering what cover up this would take – four years ago somebody would realize that Hillary Clinton would never be elected President of the United States!

The attack on the U.S. consulate in Benghazi had been planned ten days in advance. This consulate was committed by al Qaeda; Muslin Brotherhood liked "Brigades of the Captive Omar Abdul Rahman (BCOAR)." Arms shipment from Benghazi to Syria was away at the time. Also, ISIS was on the rise and the predicted failure of President Obama's policy of change in Syria. The drive and plan of the BOCAR terrorists are to kill all Americans.

Four deaths transpired in Benghazi when no response was received from the Secretary of State. The Commander in Chief shortchanged the betrayal by refusing to "Cross Border Authority." This was the reason why the 130 man USMC Fast Team in Sigonella, Italy, 370 miles (one hour and 50 minutes away) and two fully armed F-16Cs in Aviano, Italy, 1044 miles away (two hours and 30 minutes away) could have saved the lives of the Americans under attack by 125 radical Islamist terrorists during the thirteen-hour fight. The bloody aftermath doomed the lives of Ambassador Stevens, two Navy Seals, and a communication specialist. Mike Morrell was an integral part in the President Obama/Secretary Clinton whitewash or cover-up.

The CIA officer Hunter Stevens as Libyan Embassy Station Chief gave his official report on the attack of the U.S. Mission in Benghazi to his superiors at CIA headquarter in Langley, Virginia on September 12, 2011. Since General Petraeus had been relieved, Mike Morrell would ultimately dishonor and seduce 57 years of respectful service of the people assigned in the Central Intelligence Agency.

Beyond the secrecy of CIA Station Report "WOOWE," is an authorized to change its content. Mike Morrell went ahead and altered this report with Susan Rice who had the gusto to present five networks with lies about the bogus attack by Radical Islamic Terrorists. Morrell really looks like Hitler probing and clarifying the word data.

The U.S. House of Representatives Permanent Select Committee on Intelligence produced a report on the Benghazi Incident. Investigative report on the terrorist attacks of the U.S. facilities in Benghazi, Libya is the subject of this document released on September 11 – 12, 2012. This report expanded the happening of these exhaustive studies that have imploded since the attack. The reports of what happened immediately after the incident helped us understand what transpired, but yet, not all that happened by sequence or by time was cluttered by unknown discrepancies. This report left many incendiary and deceivable arts that tend to evolve in time and space. This report has pointed out several items which are:

- The State Department security personnel needed resources, and equipment were unable to counter the terrorist threat – they required CIA assistance.

- CIA was not collecting or shipping arms from Liberia to Syria. The word "rebels" was not mentioned! Previous by recorded by other sources President Obama was involved with an unknown Muslim from Dallas, Texas. Ambassador Stevens was in Benghazi to deal with Syrian rebels the guns and equipment. According to the shippers aboard, the arrangement consisted of SA-7 portable SAMs. The Obama administration is libel, must answer and should be offered no greater!

Al-Qaeda and affiliated groups participated in attacks on U.S. facilities in Benghazi, yet appropriate U.S. personnel made tactical decision. How to respond or how to rescue fellow Americans?

A mixed group of al Qaeda, Islamic Maghreb in Arabian Peninsula, AlQaeda, Mohamed Jamal Network, Ansar al-Sharia, Abu Ubaidah ibn al-Jarrah battalion, participated in the attacks, along with Gaddafi loyalists.

Appropriate personnel on the ground in Benghazi made the decision to send CIA officers to rescue the State Department at the temporary mission facility. Mike Morrell changes the following of the CIA Station Chief's Report:

a. The untruthful edit made it responsible that a YouTube. Its video was the verdict that went bad.

b. He changed the word "terrorist" in the CIA Station Chief's report to "Demonstrators."

c. All references to "Al-Qaeda" were removed.

d. Morrell removed in full "Attackers were not an escalation of a demonstration."

Mike Morrell attempted to "illegally" cover-up the CIA report were it was considered unsuitable in the eyes of President Obama and Secretary Clinton. The blemished shotgun full of holes was sent back to Morrell to eliminate much of the garbage of the wounded piece. He then told Jake Sullivan from the State Department, he would be happy to create "talking points!" He then manufactured Susan Rice's script which she delivered on five television network news broadcasts!

Back at the Central Intelligence Agency he blanked and deleted the 32 Americans that were then in Benghazi. Quite a bombshell, but powerful voices kept these 32 persons within the Obama administration that were restricted of those who witnessed the assault.

The U.S. Senators heard about wrong doing that he had purged the CIA analysts report. He repeatedly lied and perjured when responding to the Congressional testimony. He should have been in jail! He has also thrown out an investigation on the Benghazi attack with the emphasis on the U.S. Mission. This was an enlargement affair which turned over unknown items that occurred during the attack.

When the Federal Bureau of Investigation (FBI) was advised by the Senate that Morrell accused them of altering the CIA Station Chief's Report, a major storm erupted within the FBI headquarters; they were furious, they confronted Morrell. He backed down and admitted it was a falsehood! He fell on his sword! Mike Morrell, expert of "liar" and "traitor" has endorsed Hillary Clinton and his endorsement is a badge of dishonor and gives Clinton's campaign credibility.

From a greater view Department Chief of Staff Jeremy Bash released a new Benghazi email which "forces that could move to Benghazi" during a terrorist attack. This contact point was only hours after the attack began. President Obama redacted the military forces available that citing the Freedom of Information Act (FOIA) that allows the holding of deliberative process data.

Defense Chief of Staff Jeremy Bash directly balked the evidence given by Secretary of Defense Leon Panetta gave out of his mouth to the Senate Armed Services Committee in February 2013. Panetta claims that the time, distance, warning of the event and such an action moved very fast that a more immediate response was necessary. This was of course after six hours attack on the U.S. Consulate in Benghazi!

From newly released data:

From Bash, after consulting with General Dempsey, General Ham and other Joint Staff, they identified forces and are spinning up as we speak. Bash continued to deploy these elements through higher command. The timing is significant based on Congress testimony by Gregory Macris, Deputy Chief of Mission of the U.S.

Embassy in Tripoli. Commensurate with the timing of the assault. He said: "If we had, or if we could, scramble, an aircraft or two over Benghazi; we would have scared them to death by getting a laser on them and annihilated them." All in all, the Special Operation forces were sent from Tripoli to Benghazi to provide support.

"The Obama administration and Clinton officials kept this hidden for years," said Judicial Watch Tom Fitton. This correlates that the military was prepared to launch immediately what would make a definite impact on the CIA annex. The Obama plus the withholding of the email is the cause of the mindboggling endeavoring to put this scandal to rest!

The final or a presumably a history of investigation report headed Secret Committee Benghazi Chairman Trey Gowdy in July 8, 2016. "Chris Stevens, Sean Smith, Glen Doherty and Tyrone Woods were heroes who gave their lives in service to our country." The committee report is about 800 pages long composed in five primary sections, the following are facts among the new facts in Part One!

- Despite President Obama and Secretary of Defense Panetta's orders, nothing was sent to Benghazi or nothing was sent almost eight hours after the attacks killed the two Americans.

- With Ambassador Stevens missing, the White House sent a 7:30 pm which contained phrases "of any deployment is made."

- The Vice Chairman of the Joint Chiefs of Staff excused himself to go home to attend or to host a dinner party which honored foreign dignitaries.

- A fleet anti-terrorism security team (FAST) sat on an airplane, changed uniforms in and out for four times!

- None of the military forces met their required deployment schedule.

- Americans that were transferred from the CIA annex to Benghazi airport were former Qadhafi loyalists.

The following facts were found in Part Two:

- Five of the ten action items from 7:30 p.m. referenced video but had no direct link with the attacks in Benghazi. The State Department had direct link in real time. They also notified Jake Sullivan and Cheryl Mills whereby they had a direct telephone line to Tripoli. Greg Hicks reported no video in Libya prior to the attacks.

- National Security Council Spokesperson sent an email to two dozen places saying President Obama and the State Department released statements this morning.

- Before the president delivered his speech, Jake Sullivan sent an email to others – the subject was not too much violence in Libya.

- Susan Rice both prepared for the appearance on Sunday with five stations after the attacks on five weekends on National TV.

- McDonough apparently told the Secure Video Teleconference (SVTS) that everyone should keep their pie-holes shut in light of the FBI systematic examination!

- Susan Rice commented on Sunday brought shock and was very worried about the emulating of untruth this has brought on our country.

- The CIA September 13, 2012 was a bogus report and full of errors. The analysis used a full week before the uprising in Benghazi.

- Rivers of emails conclude that State Department employees including Cheryl Mills, Jake Sullivan, and Huma Abedin were planning a trip to Libya in October 2012. Chris Stevens wanted a "deliverable" for the Secretary and that "deliverable" would be making a mission in Benghazi a permanent consulate.

- Ambassador Stevens noticed the security on the ground lacked massively. In August 2012 he planned a trip to the mission in Benghazi, but cancelled the visit due to Ramadan secretly reasons.

- Former Secretary of Defense Leon Panetta slow and deficient in feeling, he told the committee that "an intelligence failure" occurred with Benghazi. Mike Morrell, a former CIA Deputy Directory, stated numerous times the shrewdness of data did revert to failure prior to the Benghazi attacks.

Part IV represents the select Committee's request for witness or other human data regarding the attack. They are eager to define what President Obama has proceeded to congress, what he is still keeping in the safe, and how he prevents covering up and denies to uncover the trustworthiness of this happening!

Part V consists of 25 recommendations for the Pentagon, State Department, and Intelligence Community and for the public whose son or daughter is serving the military. This must be done to hold and defend our constitution, to ensure we do not embellish Benghazi, but we can react to any emergency that we may face.

Finally, WikiLeaks November 1, 2016, is about to link the story that Ambassador Stevens was set up because of gun-running, child abuse and illicit drug running sponsored by CIA to regime change in Liberia, using terrorists funded by these activities. This was known and was leaking out that it was only two months before the election! Ambassador Stevens had to be kept silent and Petraeus had to be in a place where Congress could not take the fifth before Congress.

In the meantime, Secretary Clinton was broadcasting Ambassador Steven's whereabouts. Clinton refused to give him cover protection. Therefore, Stevens was working for the CIA – David Petraeus (head of the CIA) would know of Steven's atrocities to protect President Obama's 2012 re-election, both had to disappear.

So, this developed for years ago, permitting President Obama to be reelected, yet a deep source in the military intelligence, let it happen!

CHAPTER 18:

HILLARY CLINTON 1990 TO PRESENT

Today you are releasing 246 pages of documents of undisclosed Office of Independent Council (OIC) which gives extensive details of the investigation of Hillary Rodham Clinton for possible charges involving Whitewater/Castle Grande misuse of land scandal.

The rumors are statements against Hillary Clinton and other members of the former Associate Attorney General are the Clinton Justice case. This data was the first release of independent counsel's prosecution memos.

On April 10, 1998 summarized crimes under investigation:

Between January 1994 and February 1996, Hillary Clinton and Webster Hubbell made sworn statements to RTC, the FDIC and to the Senate and House of Representatives. These statements showed how they became retained by the Madison Guaranty Savings and Loan. The subject remains, the reversal from the RLR. The question is, whether the statements are inaccurate, but whether the data are willfully so.

The records were presented for all OIC review of all attorneys. This showed the details of Clinton/Hubbell antics. Clinton played a significant cover-up as the Clintons fought and captured the White House. A $300,000 dollar cross-loan in the Castle Grande Episode plus an additional five records hiding in the Rose Law Firm records. In essence, 1998 went on to the senior positions as complicit in activities that were hated crimes. Page 18 of the document reveals that Clinton destroyed her personal records concerning Madison Guaranty.

The evidence in the new documents covers:

- Castle Grande. The crimes were committed in Castle Grande, a sixth separate paragraph dissection of the "lands flipping" action.

- Madison guaranty Savings and Loan, headed by Clinton; she short-changed the role she played in the state regulatory movement for corrupt savings and loans.

- Vincent Foster and the missing Rose Firm Brittany Records. After Foster's July 1993 self-inflicted death, the billing records were no matter to die it seems. Several pieces of evidence which Clinton did not reveal were found in Foster's office and removed at the time of his death.

- On July 21, Bernard Nussbaum of the White House Counsel agreed to permit two former Department of Justice to review said document in Foster's offices if they could determine cause of death. Nussbaum changed his mind and reviewed the documents and "segregated" as a personal to the Clintons.

- Hiding the Betting Records, the records were placed in a closet thirty feet from the Book room. Two years later, they were found left on the table – she has the only significant interest in them, one of three people have left the documents since creation in February 1992.

- Buying the silence of a co-conspirator. During the taped conversation in person, Hubbell acknowledges that he withheld data from the OIC.

- The Missing Draft Indictment. More than 60 pages are censored and withheld by the National Archives. Multiple sources proclaim that Clinton and Hubbell watch these pages as a full indictment of the two responders!

The National Archives which hold Clinton as a full role in the Watergate scandal. On March 9, 2015 Hickman Erving testified he wrote an indictment of Clinton. On March 19, 2015 locating records found in the Draft Indictment plus 200 pages involving the Clinton/Hubbell Draft Indictment. According to Judicial Watch they are now in covert "forcing the release" of the incitement.

On April 24, 1998 the prosecutors were persuaded that a jury would not convict Clinton. No circumstantial evidence. The new circumstantial memos are damming. While Hillary Clinton's bank fraud, obstruction and other lies in Arkansas, not doubt in the White House but accurately accelerated the suicide of Vince Foster.

HILLARY CLINTON'S E-MAIL DISPUTE

In March 2010 it became known that Hillary Clinton had abused her title, U.S. Secretary of State and had used her familiar private email. These were used on official documents, thousands of emails, which were later marked by the State Department retroactively. This element of kiosk unfolded against the backdrop of the Clinton presidential campaign and brought the House Select Committee on Benghazi. Members of Congress have alleged that her use of private messaging software and private server violated State Department original drafts and procedures. Furthermore, she damaged without repair, the federal laws and regulations regarding keeping of records. Clinton denied that.

After all the classified emails were counted, the investigation by the FBI on how Clinton handled on the server. Of the 113 emails were viewed, 113 contained classified when sent, 65 contained secret and 22 deemed top secret! It was FBI Director James Comey that unmarked that Clinton did not technically interpret what these markings meant. She signed a non-disclosure as part of gaining a security clearance and sensitive data should be considered and marked as classified if the subject is not marked as such!

In May 2016, the Office of Inspector General unleashed a document in which the State Department reviewed its email practices. The FBI said "extremely careless" and preferred no charges against her. On July 6, 2016, Attorney General Loretta Lynch concurred with the assessment. The State Department opened the probe of the email which winded up with a 58 page report of the server.

BACKGROUND
CLINTON'S USE OF BLACKBERRY

In 2009 the Clintons use the Blackberry systems with her friends and colleagues. The email account on Clinton's Blackberry was hosted in the basement of her home in Chappaqua, New York. That was not disclosed to the State Department security or senior personal. The Blackberry was subject to hacking and she was not too secure for a desktop computer. She was emailed when she flew for vulnerability when she went on a trip to Asia!

The domain names were recorded as clintonemail.com, unoffice.com and presidentclinton.com registered by Eric Hothem. This was used in her home in Chappaqua, NY, until 2013 when it was sent to a data center in New Jersey before it was located in Platte River Networks in Denver, Colorado. The server runs Microsoft Exchange 2010; however, he transmitted using the service was unencrypted which may have even be liable to interception!

Internal emails were undetected in March 2013 when a hacker "Guccifer" sent emails to Sidney Blumenthal, which he was accessing Blumenthal's account. The hacking revealed the Benghazi attack and monitored the clintonmail.com address. Blumenthal did not have a security clearance!

In the summer of 2014 a number of emails were represented by the House Select Committee on Benghazi. The State Department and Madeline Albright, which at work in the office Datto, Inc., gave 30,000 transcripts and the data to call up the document. As of May 2016 no answer has been given as to why 31,000 emails by Hillary Clinton have been or could be rescued. The *New York Times* had uncovered the private server has put out a story of Benghazi during her private server. This was known as or called "email-gate!"

The use of government leases used emails leaving Secretaries of State before Clinton, Nick Merrill, Marie Harf, John Wonderlich and Dan Metcalf gave a higher or tighter control over emails as well as preventing their notice by Congress. Metcalf assayed try to send classified messages. Jason R. Baron was strictly by the books and was described as "strictly by the books."

MAY 2016 REPORT FROM STATE DEPARTMENT
INSPECTOR GENERAL LINICK

Inspector General Steve Linick released an 83-page report about the State Department email tactics. Clinton was denied approval of her server, etc., "because of risk in doing so." She did not properly use the procedure set forth with the Federal Records Act. Clinton and fellow associates refused to speak or talk with investigators while the previous four Secretaries of State complied. The report blatantly chastised Clinton and Colin Powell for a subpar manner in which recording was maintained, as Powell used a personal email account that was for business. Inspector General Linick wrote that the no evidence threat that staff had reviewed or approved Clinton's personal system. Finally, Brian Fallow supported her claim yet the audit showed she took advantage to protect, preserve, and release her records. Her cybersecurity practices must be evaluated with more comprehensive directions.

The Hacking attempts were know in Russia as early as 2011. In 2012 a hacker in Serbia scanned Clinton's Chappaqua server. During 2014 the intrusions continued from Germany, China and South Korea.

FIT IN TO HILLARY CLINTON'S ALLEGED SAP COMPROMISE

Ed Coet an U.S. Army Intelligence who was in his last job as Chief of the Human Intelligence for the U.S. European command in Stuttgart, German. The manager of Designated Programs Manager for a Special Access Program (SAP) similar to Hillary Clinton compromised on the report of the recent State Department Inspector General account to Congress. This topic was widely distributed or presented in the news:

1. The names of each SAP should be classified Top Secret which goes too far above Top Secret.

2. SAPs are sensitive that people who own security clearance giving the Top Secret Sensitive Compartment Information (TS SCI) cannot receive SAP. If they receive access to SAP unless special introduction into SAP based on operational "must know" that exceeds all "need to know" standards.

3. Being access to "read on" a SAP, in writing you have been briefed. Having access to one SAP does not release you to another. Only qualified sensitive people know they are the most stringent and protective information in the entire United States government.

4. Top Secret SCI is maintained in a highly secure area. Special Security Offices are maintained by a Program Manager. SAP Program Managers are fewer in number but have SAPs are secured cannot be discussed or sensitive into beyond Top Secret is done.

5. To begin with a TS SCI access is begun with a special background check. Those that have a higher clearance have to pass a polygraph test. Many

admirals and generals subject to a polygraph exam who have the highest clearance, many don't know if the SAP existed!

6. Comprise of a SAP is like Hillary Clinton would result in a dangerous violation.

7. SAP information is unsecured observes with lead to life in prison depending on the severity of the felony.

If Clinton had SAP in information on her rescued server, marked or not, the FBI would certainly present and would lead to a realistic security violation. Through "prosecutorial discretion" they would have the authority to impeach her.

If President Obama were to grant a pardon he would establish a present in history as an "enemy of the state!" He, the president, would face criminal prosecution. Nobody would get away with this as it's a system of government.

If she violates the law, which she did, she would be unfit to hold private office much less the President of the United States.

Threat overseas labeled or blocked flow of the five intruders. Therefore, no American secrets to the ones who try to steal information via the computer.

Classified Information in Emails: Alleged SAP compromise in various interviews Clinton said, "I did not send classified material, and I did not receive any material that was marked or designated classified." FBI investigators found 110 classified messages, 65 were Secret, and 20 were classified when it was sent as Top Secret data! Out of 2,100 emails Clinton personally wrote 104 and her aides wrote hundreds more!

INSPECTOR GENERAL COMMENTS

The following data was revealed:

*   On June 29, 2015, 55,000 emails released found "hundreds of potential emails."

*   On July 17, 2015, several emails were not marked as classified extract one was released.

- On July 24, 2015, Linick picked 40 emails and found these were transmitted from all U.S. Intelligence agencies. This is data that should never be communicated by an unclassified personal system!

- On August 10, 2015, the only two of the emails were Top Secret/Sensitive compartment information given the classification of "TK"; for Talent Keyhole, indicating material obtained by aria or space-based imagery sources and NOFORN (No foreign nationals) a secondary source said the CIA endorsed their findings that Clinton violated the findings that concerned the North Korea nuclear weapons program.

- On January 29, 2016, would not release 22 emails because of highly security compromise would prevail.

FBI INVESTIGATION

The State Department and the Intelligence Community (IC) realized that four of these serious messages brought referral to the FBI. What is a thumb drive? Thus, all Benghazi messages as well as all source data unloaded the Clinton personal server was turned over to the FBI on August 12, 2015, included the thumb drives. A source said the thumb drive data was stored in a safe in the State Department.

On August 20, 2015, U.S. District Judge Emmitt G. Sullivan ordered that Hillary Clinton's private server was in direct conflict with government policy. He also said the Platte River Networks, the Denver, Colorado server, had no knowledge of the server being copied clean, and cannot be recovered!

May 2016 FBI Director James Comey stated that Clinton's description of a probe as "a security inquiry" was wrong. The Director remarked he was conducting an investigation, that's what we do! In late June 2016 Bill Clinton met with Attorney General Loretta Lynch on her private plane. Who knows what was said. Her remarks are, social conversation, but she said the FBI is investigating whether Hillary Clinton is being charged on the use of her private email server as Secretary of State. On July 1, 2016, we will accept the FBI recommendation regarding her use of a personal email server.

Hillary Clinton maintained she did not send or receive confidential emails from her server. On a Democratic debate with Bernie Saunders on February 4, 2016, she denied sending or receiving any classified data. On a *Meet the Press* interview on July 2, 2016, she declared she had never, repeat, never received or sent emails for many months including sent any material that was marked classified.

What a bunch of fluff! For thirty years and counting, she has been practicing deception, fraud, double-dealing, subterfuge, and trickery about any subject she brings up or is required to answer about subject!

Whenever Hillary Clinton was asked a question, appeared at a House of Representatives or required a definitive answer, she turned to her Special Government Employee(SGE), Huma Abedin for advice. As Secretary of State she personally signed authorization of her as deputy chief of staff. This now involves certification, it was not done, did not produce financial disclosures and other documents of transition of the former Representative Anthony Weiner! Meanwhile, Huma Abedin was given a Top Secret clearance renewal of her SGE position!

Hillary Clinton's personal secretary, Huma Abedin is the major link to our closset enemies, slyly coordinated with a fabrication of radical Muslims; she finances global terror, including Al-Qaeda which murdered 3,000 people in 9/11. She is of Saudi Arabian descent and climbed up to be Hillary Clinton's personal secretary. This represent her network which begins with the 9/11 attacks.

Judge Sullivan reopened the case about Clinton email games which involved Abedin's "special" job appointment for an office. It reminded her of the fact that she must produce key sections of her employment. She failed to produce key element of records. She also lacked disclosures that Abedin and Weiner failed to complete:

Schedule B Part 1 – sales, exchange by you
Schedule B Part 2 – gifts, travel, etc.
Schedule C Part 2 – report your agreements

These core ethics were simply ignored by Hillary Clinton's protégé.

After a few weeks the pot blew off the kettle as the financial disclosure violated current rules. Hillary Clinton's signed authorization for rule as a SGE. Not as a working secretary she was double-dipping outside clients. Not at last was her working with questionable investigative reports deciding the Tenco. All in all, the ins and outs of Clinton's & Abedin's circle the globe with the FBI reviewing all withheld from the public.

CHAPTER 19:

TRUMP VS. CLINTON VS. OBAMA

The situation now is whether they assist him or will they let him be president? Donald Trump, why is the Congress shutting up and numerous people are getting nervous? Barack Obama, Valerie Jarrett, Eric Holder, Hillary Clinton and Jon Corzine about the holy statement between big government such as big business and other media. All for one, all for all! Who are the liars of the administration?

Everyone dreamed of being filthy rich but for the U.S diversion people. The over the top blowout has been very swift and angry. Donald Trump can self-fund. This is contagious to Trump because it is a joke! Trump has many headaches; that he behaves the "old boys club" are ready to eliminate Trump. If you are backed by stock owners, such as, George Soros, who owned Hillary Clinton with multiple donations from the Clinton Foundation.

The run-of-the-mill problems are run by foreign tickets but not George Soros or the United Auto Workers or the optimistic international or Bar Association. Donald Trump doesn't need their help – does not like the media and corporate elites dream up. This creates a dangerous dilemma for Trump since he has a huge threat as anybody can ruin everything for bribed, soiled slave masters.

Why did the GOP not impeach President Obama? John Boehner and Mitch McConnell each talk a big game. Obamacare or clearly President Obama's executive action or illegal aliens' controversy, this is ridiculous! The action warrants that the Republicans are being bribed or possibly blackmailed! In the case one is having affairs, secretly gay or stealing money.

National Security Agency, Security Exchange Commission, and the Internal Revenue Service watch every Republican figure. They survive everything "racist," President Obama's crimes, or even demand his impeachment. If you are a "good boy," you have a $5 million a year job waiting. Win or lose the million a million game!

Trump does not imbibe with this modus operandi! If he wins the election he destroys all the rules of the party. He knows his publically questioned President Obama's birth certificate, his college record, and how a mediocre student got accepted to the Ivy League! Now he is doing things such as the border is opening Mexico, illegal aliens commit violence across the border, and why are the trade deals so bad with Mexico, Russia and China?

Trump knows that the American workers always get shafted! Billions of dollars were given in a rigged no-bid contract to friends of Michelle Obama, whereby to build the defective Obamacare website. That's only $5 billion when you compare it to the deficit of $20 billion, this country is under?

Trump will see to it that:

- President Obama's architects charged for fraud by selling it by lying

- Investigation of President Obama's IRS conspiracy

- President Obama's college records

- President Obama and Clinton's for fraud comments to cover up Benghazi

- Fraud committed by the Labor Department with the "made up number" in the previous job report before the 2012 election?

President Obama needs the media to deny Trump from president of the United States. President Obama has committed many enemies. As president he can analyze the "cooked books" and records. He and all the doer's of his staff could be in prison. Hillary Clinton may go as well as 32,000 emails, lying about Benghazi, and the $6 billion "misplacing" of the money as Secretary of State.

The more they try, the more Trump will investigate each narrow crank for everyone involved. The left and the right will stymie him but they cannot intimidate him. Trump tells the truth and we will hear this truth until election time in November and in January 2017 when he arrived as president.

November 8, 2016, the election of Hillary Clinton and Donald Trump for president elect was held. By virtue of an unknown non-politician against the woman politician, was quite a turnout. Trump swept the voters by running key states and left Clinton dragging behind. His in-depth knowledge, and personal dedication showed this county needs a dedicated business. The United States is suffering from lack of jobs and some Americans are leaning on social security. Trump visited four and always five difficult states with rough crowds. He is offering a change and the cheering crowds know it. With the Supreme Court vacancy his choice, the mending of Obamacare, the generals and admirals with change. The increase of tanks, ships, aircrafts, submarines and put back the men who honor and protect our country!

VICE PRESIDENTIAL CANDIDATE SENATOR TIM KAINE

1. Hillary Clinton has selected Tim Kaine as the Vice Presidential candidate. Hillary Clinton considered numerous men but she wanted a man that was familiar with current policies and behaviors. Senator Kaine's background has climbed up from lawyer to the Senate of the Congress. He has understood the problems we faced in jobs, unemployment, Congress problems in getting a bill passed, and the problems of the east and his downright dislike of Israel!

2. Breitbart was reminded about how he criticized Hillary Clinton's Vice President, Tim Kaine. Senator Kaine is among the top anti-Israel senators. He among others designated himself by walking out on Benjamin Netanyahu's historic speech warning Congress against the so-called Iran deal.

3. Senator Kaine's record on the Islamic threat in the U.S.A. is far worse as we know it. Senator Kaine appointed a radical jihad to the Virginia Immigration Commission. Esam Omeish described by federal prosecutor in 2008 country "as the overt arm of the Muslim Brotherhood in America." Omeish is from a radical mosque that had Al-Qaeda Anwar Al-Awlaki as its imam. Two of the shooters on 9/11 hijacked and Nidal Hasan where in the mess as Hasan was the instigator for the Fort Hood shooting.

4. Senator Kaine opens the door with Jamal Barzinji who presents Global Muslin Brotherhood which he describes as a founding father of the U.S. Muslim Brotherhood.

5. What is amazing about Senator Kaine's relationship is a truly chilling moment of truth reveals an indictment of Al-Arian. The jihadist strategy is to "seek support from influential individuals, in the United States under the guise of promoting and protecting Arab rights!" This and other hilarious practice showers an assertive push to use civil rights advocacy to influence politicians. This shows Senator Kaine attending his fourth annual dinner. He thanked his friends that organized the meal and also that the audience for helping him in his campaign of Lieutenant Governor of Virginia, and Governor and asked them for help in his Senate campaign.

6. Clinton's choice revealing her choice as president to follow President Obama's policy of promoting the Muslim Brotherhood, Iran and betraying Israel. The *New York Sun* realizes the he fully backed the Obama-Clinton Middle East dilemma. The open negatives and aggressiveness toward our alley, Israel.

7. Another choice which may tumble Senator Kaine out of contention in his favor while Clinton is against Homeland Security! However, she has chosen a man that is willing to sweeten up to well-known terror organizations in American for cash. In other crisis in the face of danger and Donald Trump is the one, Clinton-Kaine all the imposters and friends of the jihad terrorism to the land we love, America.

This is why the president didn't go to France to show solidarity against the Muslim terrorist.

THE RUN FOR PRESIDENT 2016

Being moved over by President Obama, Hillary Clinton stalled or ended her election for president in 2012. With her allies namely, Huma Abedin, handling her executive part and holding onto their other jobs – at the Clinton Foundation, in Clinton's personal private office, and works with numerous consulting firms cemented to the Clinton family.

"This is a constant drip"… that's what the conflict of thirty years of prevaricating! The sword of Damocles means a sense of impending doom! A threat of doom such as a catastrophic threat looking over a year if Clinton wins the 2016 election! The email controversy, the flood of emails, and yet the new innuendos of the past weeks has brought news issues to the table. The news of Benghazi drops fog in the air – *13 Hours*, a book and a movie brings peoples' minds to reality.

Her savage pursuit of the email brings her single, passion of vulnerability to its critical state. This verifies that the former Secretary of State vis-a-vis, the potential Commander in Chief is the most corrupt and interesting politician in the U.S.A! She should have used her sword of Damocles which means one or more things that there is some catastrophic threat looming over her.

In her speeches she dwells on Obamacare which is headed for destruction! The rates or premiums are astronomical when figured by all states. Her plan is to revamp and adjust the premiums which may be a bogus fix. The lack of jobs and lack of working people, exacerbate the issue with high paying jobs leaving the United States. Many Americans are drawing unemployment and not looking for jobs. They lost the aptitude for a good computed day-to-day work habit.

Hillary Clinton has found a weak spot in foreign affairs. She visits, her trips to the foreign countries has been despicable! Saudi Arabia, Russia and many countries have taken the fall of an untrue leader. The examples are means, for example, Benghazi, when she lies continuously! Yes, she has been the alleged malfeasance in Washington for more than 20 years. Among others she has been called the white whale?

Another deal which Clinton has recognized was the Uranium deal with Russia. The deal was cemented yet what does this do to foreign security?

So, the presidency is trying to disorder IRS, Benghazi and emails as she goes on the campaign trail. If she was not running for President there is little doubt she would find any other targets. Tom Fitton's mouth is voracious and would capitalize, or any newsflash that would make Hillary Clinton jumpy!

In late 2011 Trump sent people to Hawaii to check on President Obama's birth certificate. This was in retort to President Obama's asking for a new certificate. This caused a crisis as several mistakes were in the two certificates. Several errors were voted and examined as strange or phony credibility. This issue passed and went underground. Donald Trump made his name as candidate for the President of the United States in mid-2015. The date June 10, 2015, was early and he was off and running.

The topics are on the country's big issues. These categories by the candidate views, Hillary Clinton vs. Donald Trump:

Hillary Clinton   **Donald Trump**

IMMIGRATION

Clinton: If Congress refuses to act, she will go under the law to further President Obama.	Trump: Mexico will have a wall and the people will come legally. Mexico will pay the bill.

Do you want to deport 11 million undocumented immigrants?
Clinton: NO   Trump: YES

Do you want to build a wall along the U.S. – Mexico border?
Clinton: NO   Trump: YES

Muslims face extra immigration hurdles?
Clinton: NO   Trump: YES

GUN CONTROL

Clinton: 33,000 American died. We are going to have comprehensive background checks to close the gun show loophole..	Trump: We have the right to self-defense; that's why we have concealed carrying weapons. This is legal in all 50 states.

Do you support gun-control measures?
Clinton: YES   Trump: NO

Increased background checks?
Clinton: YES   Trump: NO

Assault weapon ban?
Clinton: YES   Trump: NO

Do you support Center for Disease Control & Prevention to study gun control?

Clinton: YES   Trump: NO

THE WAR ON TERROR

Clinton: The use of air power is not sufficient. Air strikes should be used and combined with ground forces.	Trump: I would alleviate the ISIS in some way but use it with troops.

Do we need a significant increase in military spending?

Clinton: NO   Trump: YES

Should we topple Syrian President Bashar al-Assad?

Clinton: NO   Trump: NO

Would we work with President Putin to battle the Islamic State?

Clinton: YES   Trump: YES

Support increased military presence in other parts of the world that see increase in extremists?

Clinton: NO   Trump: UNCLEAR

Do you support greater domestic surveillance to identify extremists?

Clinton: YES   Trump: YES

TRADE

Clinton: Any trade deal has to produce jobs, raise wages, prosperity and protect our security.	Trump: I'm a free trader thus a conservative person. I believe in really smart trade, where we will put some on top!

Do you support the TPP?

Clinton: NO   Trump: NO

Do you support NAFTA and CAFTA?

Clinton: YES   Trump: NO

Do you support "free trade?"

Clinton: YES   Trump: UNCLEAR

Do you support increasing tariffs on trade partners?

Clinton: NO   Trump: YES

ABORTION

Clinton: We need to protect access to safe and legal abortion in principle and in practice.	Trump: Friends of mine were waiting for a child and it was going to be aborted. It was not aborted and became a great, great child.

Do you support keeping abortion legal?

Clinton: YES   Trump: NO
                    (Except in the case of rape, incest
                    and the life of the mother.)

Do you support abortion if the mother is at risk?

Clinton: YES   Trump: YES

Do you support abortion in the case of rape or incest?

Clinton: YES   Trump: YES

Restrictions on late-term abortions?

Clinton: YES   Trump: YES

ENTITLEMENTS

Clinton: I don't want to cut off social security; I'll defend and expand it.	Trump: I want to keep Social Security – will not cut it!

Should Social Security be cut?

Clinton: NO   Trump: NO

Should Medicare be privatized?

Clinton: NO   Trump: UNCLEAR

Should the retirement age be raised?

Clinton: NO   Trump: NO

LBGT RIGHTS

Clinton: No future generation of LGBT Americans that embrace their full and equal rights	Trump: In New York I know many people, gay people. Tremendous people!.

Should transgender people use the bathroom that corresponds to their gender identity?

Clinton: YES   Trump: YES

Do you support same-sex marriage?

Clinton: YES   Trump: NO

ENERGY AND THE ENVIRONMENT

Clinton: Don't let anyone take you backward, deny our economy harassing a clean future or let our children endure the catastrophe of unchecked climate change.	Trump: This very extensive global warming bullshit has got to stop!

Do you believe in climate change?

Clinton: YES   Trump: NO

Should offshore drilling be banned?

Clinton: YES   Trump: NO

Should fracking be banned?

Clinton: NO   Trump: NO

Should construction of the Keystone XL pipeline resume?

Clinton: NO   Trump: YES

THE ECONOMY

Clinton: Creating good paying jobs and raising incomes and that will take us where the growth of the economy is!	Trump: I will be the greatest jobs president that God ever created!

Should the minimum wage be raised?

Clinton: YES   Trump: NO

Should taxes be raised on the wealthiest Americans?

Clinton: YES   Trump: UNCLEAR

Should the U.S. tax corporate profits stashed overseas?

Clinton: YES   Trump: YES

HEALTH CARE

Clinton: Affordable health care is a basic human right.	Trump: We are going to repeal Obamacare. Replace this program with something so much better.

Should Obamacare be replaced?

Clinton: NO   Trump: YES

Do you support the individual mandate?

Clinton: YES   Trump: NO

Should Medicaid be expanded?

Clinton: YES   Trump: NO

CRIMINAL JUSTICE

Clinton: Something is wrong between law enforcement and community break down in many of our communities.	Trump: I have to say that the police are mistrusted and misunderstood.

Do you support the death penalty?

Clinton: YES   Trump: YES

Should police body cameras be mandatory?

Clinton: YES   Trump: NO

Should minimum sentences for nonviolent drug offenders be reformed?

Clinton: NO   Trump: UNCLEAR

Should prisons be privatized?

Clinton: NO   Trump: NO

EDUCATION

Clinton: Everyone to refinance your student loans so you will never have to pay more than you can afford.	Trump: Tremendous people believe in education, but education has to be at a local level.

Do you support charter schools?

Clinton: YES   Trump: YES

Do you support Common Core?

Clinton: YES   Trump: NO

Should there be a moratorium on student debt?

Clinton: YES   Trump: UNCLEAR

CAMPAIGN FINANCE

Clinton: We need a Supreme Court that says no to Citizens United, that decision that has undermined the election system in our country.	Trump: These super PACs are a disaster, by the way, it's very corrupt. It's going to lead to many disasters.

Should Citizens United decision be overturned?

Clinton: YES   Trump: UNCLEAR

Do you support more disclosure of political spending?

Clinton: YES   Trump: UNCLEAR

Do you support public financing?

Clinton: YES   Trump: UNCLEAR

Judge Waters determined that it submitted questions to Hillary Clinton regarding her email habit. The answers, under oath, will be provided by September 29, 2016. District Court Judge Emmett G. Sullivan ordered Clinton no later than thirty days thereafter. The questions were very sacrosanct and were to be answered in fact with honesty and truth.

On October 14, 2016, the twenty-five questions were returned to the Judicial Watch with she "does not recall" twenty times. These new responses were reviewed under the Freedom of Information Act (FOIA) lawsuit before Judge Sullivan which was filed in September 2013. This was trying to establish records pertaining to the employment of Huma Abedin former deputy chief of staff to Clinton. This most obviously was reopened because of disclosing about the clintonemail.com.

The twenty emails that she "does not recall" basically denies none of the specific decision for use of the clintonemail.com account for official State Department transactions.

What a blow to security! Hillary Clinton's blatant failures of mind and brain are typical of the fact that she fears full disclosure of her emails. Judicial Watch President Tom Fitton agrees with this statement!

On November 9, 2016, the name of the president-elect was known – Donald Trump. The sates in particular, Florida, North Carolina, Pennsylvania, Michigan and Wisconsin went Trump all the way. This caused the Republican winner the lead for votes but won the state vote as a dominant figure. Hillary Clinton won the popular vote, so what! Trump was paramount in happiness and accepted the honor and prestigious fame at three o'clock in the morning amid his whole family.

In view of the many projects laid out, president-elect must begin digging out the U.S. government infiltrators and to crush them. January 21, 2017, he must give the go-ahead to a top-secret operation to destroy Muslim spies and to disable their ISIS overlords keeping in American. On November 12 Homeland Security Agency (HSA) and Central Intelligence Agency (CIA) delivered to Trump a dossier exposing 55 spies who have penetrated all levels of U.S. government. Code-named, "Deep Cleanse," which President Trump starts after the inauguration. This false led convert cognizant will cause false database that confuse ISIS. This possible should let the leaks can destroy ISIS. CIA and has worked covertly for 18 months to root out 55 jihadist suspicious traitors in our secret fire side palace! One Pentagon whistle blower accepted the threat of American forces.

U.S. Admiral James Al. Lyons accused President Obama as playing tootsie with Islamic terrorists of being "anti-American, pro-Islamic, pro-Iranian and pro-Muslim Brotherhood." Lyons states that we have a hard row to hoe. This will contain all national security interest and all intelligence.

President Obama was born in Hawaii (not proven to be true) and lived in Indonesia from the age of six to ten. In Indonesia he read the Koran and remains a secret this day of being a Muslim. The intelligence czars confirmed 42 confirmed deep covert Islamists. By monitoring e-mail, phone records, photos and through social matters, in these cases video surveillance caught the backstabbers red-handed! Thirteen other incidents lack ironclad proof. Still the 55 suspects remain under the claw of the intelligence tiger. Homeland Security and CIA were given who conducted six month probe exposing White House staffers as ISIS members in 2015. The Oval Office convened a 90-minute mutiny which told President Obama of the Muslim menace under the crack of his door to his top-secret office.

FBI turncoat, Robert Hanssen, was exposed in 2001. This provides a lesson which embellished the traitors to be condensed on the intelligence experts. They must be aware that they are using techniques of torture – including waterboarding. They have already informed President-elect Trump of reviewing this procedure. They have also prompted Trump to keep captured terrorists at U.S. Guantanamo, Cuba. The word around Washington is the president-elect will keep Guantanamo open and begin extreme interrogations.

CHAPTER 20: BARACK HUSSEIN OBAMA

EIGHT YEARS OF DESPAIR

The President Barack Hussein Obama took office in 2009 and started with naming his cabinet, the czars. The czars were the answer to the troublesome actions of the United States. Very few of the population know their names, where they are or what they stand for. There were thirty-two persons that had the responsibility of going forward or backward! Anthony K. "Van" Jones, graduated from school at Yale University, received a "well done" by the elect team, and was later honored by the selection of *Time* as the most influential person in the U.S.A.!

In March 2009 Jones became part of the staff and was appointed Council on Environmental Quality Special Advisor for green jobs. In July 2009 he became radical which began pleasing him. He made a blatant comment about Republicans and, therefore, joined a Marxist group which he joined in 1990. He resigned in September 2009. You wonder what the members of Czar were up to!

One of the problems that President Obama brought to light was being accountable. According to the Merriam-Webster dictionary, "accountable: 1. Subject to giving an account; answerable, 2. capable of being accounted for: explainable." Another problem area is decade! When one speaks of decade it means a group of sets of 10s. In other discourse, it means a period of ten years. So it is not polite to carry on a conversation using decade when one is describing the exact year the event happens!

Another catchphrase which the President Obama inevitably uses is: "going forward." Now technically it is used concerning passage of a bill, going forward with the process. Why not use move or proceed with the action?

President Obama recently admitted that he had prided himself by having no scandals in the last eight years. This was countermanded by Valerie Jarrett – she underscored his position. Jarrett is his right-hand person, she being from Iran. Does that joggle your thoughts about the president being a Muslim? President Obama did not admit he has salacious scandals, but they are there troubling him. Valerie Jarrett admits we had no problem or scandals during our eight years as the White House advisor. She has, although not mentioned, she has the broadest and most collective roles in the West Wing. She, for example, was at Martha's Vineyard with the president. Denis McDonough, the chief of staff, was not there! Valerie Jarrett was there for eight years "to help change American to be a more Islamic country!"

The scandals that engross his attention are:

1. Operation Fast and Furious
2. Benghazi
3. IRS targeting conservatives
4. DOJ Targeting
5. NSA mass surveillance
6. Ransom pay to Iran
7. Bowe Bergdahl
8. Secret Service scandal
9. Clinton Email scandal

NINE CONTROVERSIES OF PRESIDENT OBAMA

There have been eight years of things that did not set well with President Obama. A look at the nine controversies that have beleaguered the president are:

1. Fast and Furious: On December of 2009 the operation took place under the ATF took charge and wound up shooting Border Patrol tactical team Brian Terry. Next to Terry were weapons traced to the Lone Wolf Trading Company. An arrest was made with two of the weapons with nineteen suspects detained. Finally, on December 16, 2010, the 350-count of weapons were recovered. This put the cap on the Fast and Furious investigation.

2. Benghazi: The question will have evolved about how President Obama handled the terrorist attack at the U.S. Consulate in Benghazi, Liberia.

The pressure and the use of various techniques to cover-up this bodacious incident has somehow escaped the media, investigative team and remains a White House scare. Of course, this was downplayed links to Islamic militants in the initial beginning of the start of the raid on Benghazi.

3. Internal Revenue Service (I.R.S.) targeting conservatives: The IRS scandal of 2013 is the Internal Revenue Service had detected that it had targeted conservative and Tea Party groups for extra security before the presidential election in 2012. The fallout was fierce and led to numerous resignations of head department.

4. Department of Justice targeting: The Department of Justice (DOJ) secretly moved and obtained telephone records of editors and reports with service of those who worked for the Associated Press in 2012. This move was described as a leak in the last probe. The journalists were beside themselves and were furious! They called the apprehending of the intrusion into the lifeblood of the A.P.'s gathering of news. Attorney General Eric Holder's Justice Department secretly or covertly obtained two months of telephone records of which journalists were the victim!

5. National Security Agency (N.S.A.) Mass Surveillance: They had been using a spy aggregate center in Bluffdale, Utah. Reported near Salt Lake City, it has the largest spy collection center in the world. It also has the most prominent computer power processer. The N.S.A. has been suing a "super-secret" computer which collects emails, video pictures, and data on major United States internet businesses' websites. They often capture those transmitted by unsuspected Americans without proof in the call of national security. This program was declared unconstitutional by a federal judge during President Obama's second term.

6. Ransom pay to Iran: A day after the compact deal with Iran, the nuclear program was implemented in January 2016. In the meantime, the United States paid $1.7 billion to settle an old unfinished business with Iran. Presto magic, the Iran Republic let loose four Americans that it had held in prison. The timing was dismal and it had the aura of a ransom payment. The White House denied it, but it was impossible to deny that the white

House paid the regime in exchange for the liberty of four U.S. citizens! Be it known that the Obama administration paying off the regime that has been kidnapping and killing Americans for 37 years of their existence!

7. Bowe Bergdahl: Army Sergeant Bowe Bergdahl left his post in Afghanistan in 2009. President Obama exchanged five Guantanamo Bay prisoners in 2009 to get Bergdahl back to the United States. "For do not ever leave our men and women in uniform behind." After 30 years of age, he is charged with desertion. A military judge decided in August 2016 to delay his trial to February 2017 in order to review his classified documents.

8. Secret Service scandal: The agency of Secret Service has been begging to rescue it from unbelievable high-profile mistakes. Yet this bureaucracy is facing another crisis. The first incident happened in April 2, 2015, and Joe Clancy was given a synopsis of the event. Last month a possible bomb altered the fence. Earlier a fence jumper gained access to the East Room of the White House. There is no justification for this happening. The director Joe Clancy states that we must facelift a trust within our force and we must protect the White House.

9. Clinton email scandal: To a former State Department and the emails she has generated, there is no excuse to have them generate classified material. Hillary Clinton has breached the Special Access Program which has violated the classification of emails and must be tried in court.

KEYSTONE XL PIPELINE SUMMARY

The Keystone XL Pipeline cost the environmental money when President Obama spent during the second term. The administration was reviewing claims that supported the pipeline which carries additional new jobs, perhaps thousands, would be the result of his project when delivered. Opponents argued that the environmental impact would increase pollution which would lead to global warming.

The Keystone XL Pipeline is under the leadership of the Canadian company Trans Canada. The first phase will carry oil from Canada to the Gulf of Mexico. The pipeline will transport about 1,179 miles from Canada to Steele City, Nebraska. The Department of State weighs a number of issues regarding approval prior to granting a permit. President Obama relished a firm believer in climate change and has refused to grant acceptance of the Keystone project. Donald Trump is expected to authorize this pipeline when he takes over the presidency.

In view of this disgust, President Obama will leave a plate full of delinquent bodacious vegetables on his plate. The things that also bother him are the Keystone XL Pipeline controversy and Obamacare. President Obama promised to spend time to analyze the cause of global warming. The Bible states that God controls the weather. There is nothing, no evidence that suggests that we can control the weather. We were given dominion over the earth and all that is in it, but not the entire universe. The problem with Obamacare – it's extensive! Those who sub-scribe to these plans, all struggling to keep up with the design.

President Barrack Obama prided himself in being a speaker although with an "a-a-a" phrase which irritated myself. He has abused over the Congress and the government. In his legacy the distribution of aggregative power is the headline of success. There is one characteristic that will go down in the White House; there is a man that frequents him behind closed doors!

Presidential gifts are taken fairly often. Judicial Watch has obtained figures from both the Secret Service and the Air Force regarding the travel expense of Obamas; the known total is $96,938,882.51!

The Secret Service records the following:

- Florida Everglades - $1,45,752.36 April 22, 2015

- President Obama's fundraising $180,787.06 October 2015

- Michele Obama ski trip to Aspen $222,875.58 Feb 2016, Secret Service $165,806.78

- President Obama's trip to Morocco, Spain & Liberia June 2016 $450,026.40

- President Obama's vacation to Martha's Vineyard, August 2016 $450,295

- Hilary Clinton to North Carolina, October 2016 $26,522.80

The Obama trips have caused a great deal of concern and wasted military re-sources. The trips or vacations to Hawaii have not been assessed. This is estimated that the expenditure of funds will exceed $100 million dollars. Clearly we must put immediately a stop and reform presidential waste or travel!

Every American President except President Obama has taken the time to honor the sacrifices of 6,000 American soldiers killed on D-Day!

CHAPTER 21:

EPILOGUE

This president was turned into the once respected U.S.A. into a joke, reduced Congress into a laughing group, turns the finest medical plan into a third rate country with a stroke of a pen, our Constitution was taken and used to write a document and turn our once nimble, succinct U.S.A. into a group of competing, divided vulgar voices.

Many people are worried about the advice the president gets from day to day for eight years, conservative national incidents. There's Valerie Jarrett, Eric Holder, Susan Rice, Hillary Clinton and Jon Corzine. Senior advisor Valerie Jarrett, overseeing the White House of both public and inter-government affairs, she was born in Iran which is where her thoughts transpire. She states that she is Islamic faith. She holds a strategic vote on the cabinet picks and has her say on ambassadorships and judges. She yields too much control over the president because she is a foreign born Islamic "mole" for a Muslim agenda through the executive board.

Susan Rice is a United States cabinet member in the Obama administration as the country's ambassador to the United Nations Born in Washington, D.C., she studied at Stanford and went to the University of Oxford in England. In 2009 she affiliated to President Obama's cabinet as the United Nations ambassador. In 2013 she became the National Security Advisor for President Obama. Rice accompanies the president on diplomatic trips. I wonder why she travels with President Obama on all trips to foreign countries.

Hillary Clinton has a right to be included, but that involved the emir incident, Benghazi falsehoods, and the president also had dispersion of wrong emails.

President Obama's last act could be the attack on Israel. This form of betrayal stymies from a voting on anti-Israel United Nations (U.N.) resolution. This is according to Islamic to "craft and punish it."

Resolution 2324 which has reversed U.S. policy assists the Palestinians in their legal war against Israel. It avoids direct negotiation, supports international conflict by bringing about boycotts and raising sanctions forcing them. It takes more than a resolution to make it happen. Furthermore, it states that the West Wall is Palestine territory and the Jews living there are illegally occupied.

The surprising part is that President Obama is in support of the U.N. action. In addition he has intervened in Israel's election to defeat the prime minister, Benjamin Netanyahu. President Obama, "a man on the left," has shown time and time again his promise of anti-Israel reflexes. He likes to say as he overlooks or ridicules the malevolence of his military adversaries.

In an extraordinary rising undertaken the United States has directed enmity against one of the most loyal and history's most admirable. Israel is a democratic, self-critical and is loved by human and major rights. It reels of war over has made sacrifices for peace. President Obama and those on the left are pushing an old narrative that voted in tenth-distortions are inaccessible as they are done to weaken the Jewish state.

The U.S. has been an anti-Israel and anti-Semite state. Obama continues to stand and it is a monument that is sordid as it was conditional.

PAYMENT TO PALESTINE

Freeze on President Obama's $221 million payment to Palestine

President Obama, quietly as a cat, gave Palestine $221 million dollars just hours before the Trump inauguration ceremony. The State Department will investigate and shut or stop payment while it investigates payment if it's inappropriate. The action will look at this payment although it is one of the final acts of President Obama.

The outright payment was frozen by Congress by questioning of the Palestine Authority. President Obama was bound by either Arab or Custom pledge did not appreciate the freeze, violated this act by signing this document. A woman Republican stopped this payment and was infuriated with President Obama's act.

American tax dollars would not give Palestine necessary funding or will not grant these dollars that go to programs not under review by the Congress. This is typical of the Obama administration for the past eight years of office. The easy and most algebraic method to make unilateral attempts at statehood, violent, corruption and paying salaries to persons held for terrorist – is reason for the hold on the money!

The clandestine move by President Obama may be viewed as a strike against Israel. Trump has made a pretentious display of showing support for Israel because it strengthens its claim over the old city, Jerusalem.

Since 1920s Russian communists have tried to tear apart the United States' elections. Interestingly, they are trying without success in France. The ultimate goal of elections is to erratic the Russians, Cuba and especially the Muslim Brotherhood, defeating foreign powers from bending U.S. Congressional or presidential elections.

Hillary Clinton was onboard with the liberal media which has been promoting Russian enemy traits as why she lost the election! Clearly it is said that Russia communicated via the Trump Presidential Campaign to hack to involve and deny her right to be president.

"The Duplicity of the Russian Collusion" is the conclusion between President Obama, Democrat Senators, and the Russians. The Russia narrative is a ridiculous liberal media in order to destroy the prestige of Trump. Collusion – a secret agreement, there is no evidence or anyone can prove it. The Director of National Intelligence in the Obama management, James Clapper stated no one in the Russia hierarchy that attended the votes and hindered Hillary Clinton to lose this race.

Organize for America (OFA), President Obama's leftist and progressive fronts has Soros, Bill Ayers, and Valerie Jarrett (who moved into Obama's rented house) to initiate a coup d'état to boot the President out of office. President Obama likes Trump – no! President Obama and Soros are employing 32,000 Alinsky radicals, with 250 offices across the United States paid by Soros to dump the Trump administration. The ex-president puts on a smiling "sunshine smile" for the press. President Obama has, until the cabinet is filled, many thousands of workers in the U.S. government, intelligence agencies and other departments of the government.

A review of the duplicity by President Obama, Hillary Clinton, Valerie Jarrett, and Democratic Senators and Congressman was overlooked and ignored by "the left of center" liberal media for eight years. The true "Russian Collusion" is between Barack Obama, the Obama administration, Hillary Clinton, and the Russians. Obama, a former occupant of the Oval Office, has tried to sabotaging Trump's one hundred days on a daily basis.

As President-elect Donald trump in two weeks takes control of the presidency, he and the members of his staff will solve the battles before him. He should as he already has in mind, the Israel issue, numerous presidential executive orders, Obamacare, jobs and many more items which affect the economy. We as American citizens are bound to support and may he achieve the high caliber of excellence!

Goodbye to a poor individual that has been his name fall in its descent. The Commander in Chief departs, but the failure of Benghazi falls strictly on his head and the ability to lead a mighty nation the United States of America!

CHAPTER 22:

END NOTES

Books by and About General Douglas MacArthur,
hhtp://www.quoteland.com/author/General-Douglas-MacAuthur-
Quotes/1337/?pg=1,12/12/2016

The War To End Wars-1911- 1918, Reader Digest Association, Pleasantville,
NY, 2000

World War 2, http://worldwar-2,into/summary,

World War Two-Causes, http://www.historyonthenet.com/WW2/causes.htm, August 14, 2014

USS North Carolina (BB-55), Wikipedia, the free encyclopedia, hhtp://
en.wikipedia.org/wiki/USS North Carolina_(BB-55), February 1, 2016

Attack on Pearl Harbor – Wikipedia, the free encyclopedia, http://
en.wikipedia.org/wiki/Attack on Pearl Harbor, February, 2016

The Legend of the Kamikaze: Suicide Bombers in World War 2 – InfoBarrel,
http://www.infobarrel.com/The_of_the_Kamikaze_Suicide_Bombers_in_W
orld, March 23, 2016

United States Navy in World War II, Wikipedia, the free encyclopedia,
http://en.wikipedia.org/wiki/United_States_Navy_in_World_War_II, January 27, 2016

World War 2 –Summary, http://world-war-2.info/summary, November 3, 2015

SOSUS Unclassified Cover Story, http://www.iusscaa.org/coverstory.htm, January 3, 2017

Integrated Undersea Surveillance System (IUSS) History 1950 – 2010, http://www.iusscaa.org/history.htm, January 3, 2017

Korean War- Fact & Summary, http://wwww.history.com/topics/korean-war, February 15, 2016

Teaching With Documents: The United States Enters the Korean War, http://www.archives.gov/education/lessons/korean-conflict/, February 22, 2016

President Truman's relief of General Douglas MacArthur, http://en.wikipedia.org/wiki/President_Truman%27s_relief_of_General_Douglas_MacArthur. February 20, 2017

Vietnam War, http://www.britannica.com/event/Vietnam-War, March 22, 2016

History of the Taliban: Who They Are, What They Want, http://middleeast.about.com/od.afghanistan/ss/me080914a.htm, July 12, 2016

Afghanistan War, http://www.britannica.com/event/Afghanistan-War, July 8, 2016

ISLAM: Religion of Peace or War? http://www.cbn.com/noindex/PPC/Islam-Religion-of-Peace-or-War-b.pdf., 2014 Published by the Truth

The Terrorist Threat Confronting the United States, hhtp://archives.fbi.gov/archives/news/testimony/the-terrorist-threat-confronting-the-unite..,October27, 2016

Explaining Boko Haram, Nigeria's Islamist Insurgency, http:www.nytimes.com/2014.11.11/world/Africa/boko-haram-in-nigeria-.html? r=1, August 10, 2016

Al-Qaeda in the Arabian Peninsula, http://en.wikipedia.org/wiki/Al-Qaeda_in_the_Arabian_Peninsula, August 10, 2016

History of the Taliban: Who They Are, What They Want, http://middleeast.about.com/od/afghanistan/ss/me080914a.htm, July 12, 2016

National Counterterrorism Center I Groups, Hamas, http://www.nctc.gov/site/groups/hamas.html, August 28, 2016

BBC News – Who are Hamas?, http://news.bbc.co.uk/2/hi/1654510.stm, August 29, 2016

Sobel, Jerrold L, There Was Never a Country Called Palestine, http://americanthinker.com/articles/2012/02/there_was_never_a_country_called_pal, February 12, 2016

Who Are Hezbollah?, http://news.bbc.co.uk/2/hi/middle_east/4314423.stm, September 6, 2016

Factors that Led to the Iraqi Invasion of Kuwait,
http://www.indepthinfo.com/iraq.shtml, May 5, 2016

The Gulf War – Kuwait, http://.indepthinfo.com/iraq/kuwait.shtml, May 1, 2016

The Saudi Invitation, http://www.indepthinfo.com/iraq/invitation.shtml, May 1, 2016

U S Interests in the Gulf War, http://www.indepthinfo.com/iraq,interests.shtml, May 23, 2016

Build Up of Forces, http://www.indepthinfo.com/Iraq/builtup.shtml, May 1, 2016

Air War – Operation Desert Storm,
http://www.indepthinfo.com/Iraq/airwar.shtml, May 1, 2016

The Ground War – Operation Desert Storm,
http://www.indepthinfo.com/iraq/groundwar.shtml, May 23, 2016

Aftermath of the Gulf War, http://www.indeptinfo.com/iraq/afermath.shtml, May 23, 2016

Singal, Jesse; Limm, Christine and Stephey – Seven Years in Iraq: An Iraq War Timeline,
http://content.time.com/time/specials/packages/article/0,28804,1967340,196 7350,196745, 6/25/2016

ISIS trail of Terror Is ISIS a Threat to the U.S.? – ABC News,
http://abcnews.go.com/WN/fullpage/isis-trail-terror-isis-threat-us-25053190, 11/2/2016

Gilsinan, Kathy, The Confused Person's Guide to the Syrian Civil War,
http://www.theatlantic.com/international/archive/2015/10/Syrian-civil-war-guide-isis/410, October 29, 2015

Judicial Watch: New Benghazi Email Shows DOD Offered State Department "Forces that Could Move to Benghazi" Immediately – Specifics Blacked Out in New Document, http://www.judicialwatch.org/press-room/press-releases/judicial-watch-new-benghazi-email-shows-dod-offered-state-department-forces-that- could-move-to-b, 12/8, 2015

John, Capt Joseph R., Ex-CIA Deputy Appointed by Obama, Lied, and Whitewashed Benghazi Murders, Now He Endorses Hillary,

http://mail.google.com/mail/u/0/?ui=2&ik=0b94c40bf1&view=pt&search=s
ent&th=1566c22d46165b29&simi=1566c22d46165b29, August 8, 2016

Ibid.

Select Committee on Benghazi Releases Proposed Report,
http://benghazi.house.gov/NewInfo, 10/6/2016

Judicial Watch Changes History On Benghazi,
http://mail.google.com/mail/u/0/?ui=2&ik=Ob94c40bf1&view=pt&search=
inbox&th=1509788af15eeb6d&siml=1509788af15eeb6d, 10/23/2015

Gmail-Weekly Update: JW WANTS Action on Clinton Emails, Another Benghazi Breakthrough,
http://mail.googe.com/mail/u/O/?ui=2&ik=Ob94c40bf1&view=pt&search=i
nbox&th=14dc6952e040748c&simi=14dc6952e040748c, June 5, 2015

Benghazi Lies Began With Obama and Hillary,
http://mail.googe.com/mail/u/O/?ui=2&ik=Ob94c40bf&view=pt&search=in
box&th=14e545ca16f4906&simi=14e545fca16f4906, July 6, 2015

Judicial Watch Proves Clinton Knowingly Lied about Benghazi,
http://mail.google.com/mail/u/O/?ui=2&ik=Ob94c40bf1&view=pt&search=
inbox&th=151032Ob29c6295a&simi=1510320b29c6295a, November 13,
2015

Harris, Shane, The Lawyers Who Could Take Down Hillary Clinton's Campaign, http://www.thedailybeast.com/articles/2016/06/20the-lawyers-who-
could-take-down-hillary-clinton-campaign.html?via=twitter_page,
10/17/2016

Whitewater Controversy, http://en.wikipedia.org/wiki/Whitewater_controversy,
March 23, 2016

Hillary Clinton email controversy, http://en.wikipedia.org/wiki/Hillary_Clin-
ton_email_controversy, November 16, 2016

Fitton, Tom, Judicial Watch: New State Department Records Reveal Clinton
Aide Abedin Secured State Dept. Lunch Invitation for Major Clinton Foundation Donor, http://www.judicialwatch.org/press-room/press-releases/judi-
cial-watch-new-state-department-records-reveal-clinton-aide-abedin-secure
d-state-dept-lunch-invitation-for-major-, 2/12/2017

Judicial Watch Puts Hillary Clinton on the Spot over Abedin Patronage Job,
http://mail.google.com/mail/u/O/?ui=2&ik=Ob94c40bf1&view=pt&search=
inbox&th=15006bf4d47725a57SIML=15006BF4D47725A5, September 25,
2016

Coet, Ed, What all Americans need to know about Hillary Clinton's alleged SAP compromise –Maj Ed Coet, USA (RET), http://mail.google.com/mail/u/O/?ui=2&ik=Ob94c40bf1&view=pt&search=sent&th=152a43ea4c96fec4&simi=152a43ea4c96fec4, February 2, 2016

Jaccarino, Mike, Huma's Web of Terror Exposed, *National Enquirer*, November 21, 2016

Donald Trump vs. Hillary Clinton on the issues, http://www.washingtonpost.com/graphics/political-issues, 11/27/2016

Breitbart, This man appears to be a bad, bad, bad guy, http://mail.google.com/mail/uO/?ui=2&ik=Ob94c40bf1&view=pt&search=inbox&th=156fc01b6c673c83&simi=156fc01b6c673c83, September5, 2016

Judicial Watch Submits Email Questions to Hillary Clinton – Written Answers, Under Oath, Due September 29, http://www.judicialwatch.org/press-room/press-releases/judicial-watch-submits-email-questions-hillary-clinton-written-answers-oath/due-september-29/?utm, August 30, 2016

Clinton Claims She 'Does Not Recall' 20 Times in Under Oath Responses to 25 Email Questions, http:///wwwjudicialwatch.org/press-room/press-releases/Clinton-claims-not-recall-20-times-oath-responses-25-email-questions/?utm_source=SilverpopMailin, October 14, 2016

Zezima, Katie and Callahan, Matthew, Donald Trump vs. Hillary Clinton on the issues, https://www.washingtonpost.com/graphics/politiics/political-issues, November 27, 2016

Fox News Video, Obama's Closest Advisor Says President Has Been Scandal – Free, January 3, 2017

Merse, Tom, The Biggest Controversies of Barack Obama's Presidency, http://uspolitics.about.com/od/energy/a/Keystone-Pipeline-Controversy.htm, 1/5/2017

Mikkelson,David, White House advisor Valerie Jarrett did not say she seeks "to help change America to be a more Islamic country," http://www.snopes.com/politics/quotes/jarrettislam.asp, May 22, 2016

Mikkelson, David, Susan Rice, http://www.biography.com/people/susan-rice-391616, January 8, 2017

Bowe Bergdahl court-martial delayed until February 2017, http://www.foxnews.com/us/2016/05/17/bergdahl-court-martial-wait-until-after-nove, May 17, 2016

Judicial Watch: New Obama Travel Costs Bring Eight-Year Total over $96 Million, http://www.judicialwatch.org/press-room/press-releases/judicial-watch-new-obama-travel-costs-bring-eight-year-total-96-million/?utm_source=SilverpopMaili, December 29, 2016

Bennett, Bill, According to Bill Bennett, http://google.com/mail/u/O/?ui=2&ik=Ob94c40bf1&view=pt&search=inbox&th=1530fbe5b87c94f9&simi=1530fbe5b87c94f9, 2/23/2016

Wehner, Peter, Obama's Attack on Israel, http://www.realclearpolitics.com/articles/2016/12/28/obamas_attack_on_israel_132657.html, 1/9/2017

Beckman, Shannon, Chain email falsely claims Obama is only president not to visit D-Day monument, http://www.politifact.com/truth-o-meter/statements/2014/may/30/chain-email/chain-email, May 30, 2014

Garcia, Carlos, Trump admin puts a freeze on Obama's $221 million payment to Palestinians, http://www.theblaze.com/news/2017/01/25/trump-admin-puts-a-freeze-on-obamas-221mill...,January 25, 2017

CPSIA information can be obtained
at www.ICGtesting.com
Printed in the USA
BVHW040725030319
541639BV00022B/572/P